Losing out?

Socioeconomic disadvantage and experience in further and higher education

Alasdair Forsyth and Andy Furlong

The POLICY PRESS

First published in Great Britain in May 2003 by

The Policy Press
Fourth Floor, Beacon House
Queen's Road
Bristol BS8 1QU
UK

Tel no +44 (0)117 331 4054
Fax no+44 (0)117 331 4093
E-mail tpp-info@bristol.ac.uk
www.policypress.org.uk

© University of Glasgow
Transferred to Digital Print 2004

Published for the Joseph Rowntree Foundation by The Policy Press

ISBN 1 86134 508 9

Alasdair Forsyth is Research Associate in the Department of Sociology and Anthropology, University of Glasgow and **Andy Furlong** is Professor of Sociology and Head of the Department of Sociology and Anthropology, University of Glasgow.

The **Joseph Rowntree Foundation** has supported this project as part of its programme of research and innovative development projects, which it hopes will be of value to policy makers, practitioners and service users. The facts presented and views expressed in this report are, however, those of the authors and not necessarily those of the Foundation.

Cover design by Qube Design Associates, Bristol
Cover photographs kindly supplied by Alasdair Forsyth
Printed and bound in Great Britain by Marston Book Services Limited, Oxford.

Contents

Acknowledgements   iv
Preface   v
Glossary   vi

1   Socioeconomic disadvantage and experience in further and higher education: issues   1
    Introduction   1
    Inequities in participation   1
    Links to the previous project   3
    Research methods   4
    Summary   5

2   Destinations of disadvantaged school-leavers   6
    Introduction   6
    Disadvantage and prior educational attainment   7
    Disadvantage and access to post-school education   9
    Summary   10

3   Patterns of participation in further and higher education   11
    Introduction   11
    Students and non-students   12
    Student lifestyle and finance   15
    Summary   17

4   Patterns of success in further and higher education   19
    Introduction   19
    Career pathways of disadvantaged students   19
    Predicting changes in participation   23
    Summary   26

5   Barriers to full participation in further and higher education   27
    Introduction   27
    Educational disadvantage   28
    Economic disadvantage   33
    Cultural disadvantage   43
    Career disadvantage   48
    Summary   51

6   Conclusions and policy implications   52

Bibliography   57
Appendix A: 'Baseline' sample demographics   58
Appendix B: Regression equations   59
Appendix C: 'Final' sample demographics   61
Appendix D: Subjects studied   62
Appendix E: Institutions attended   63
Appendix F: Types of reduced participation   64
Appendix G: Selection of interviewees   65
Appendix H: Profiles of 2001 interviewees   66
Appendix I: Profiles of 2002 interviewees   68

Acknowledgements

The researchers would like to express their appreciation to the members of the project advisory committee: Andy Biggart, Fred Cartmel, Cathy Howieson, Charlie Lloyd, Kevin Lowden, Janice Pattie, Sheila Riddell and John Tibbit. We would also like to thank Kay Devlin for transcribing interviews. Finally thanks are also due to the young people themselves who gave up their valuable time to take part in this research.

Preface

This research project is a continuation of a previous Joseph Rowntree Foundation-funded project, which was conducted during 1999 and 2000. The previous project recruited a sample of young people during their final year of attendance at schools located in areas of disadvantage. These young people were tracked to see who among them had accessed higher education and who had not, and to gain insight regarding the career barriers faced by disadvantaged students. The present research project builds on this previous one by tracking the academic progress of these young people one stage further, on this occasion, within higher education. *It must be stressed that the young people who took part in this research are only representative of students who had previously attended secondary schools located in areas of socioeconomic disadvantage and, as such, they are not typical of, or comparable with, the student population in general.* Full details of the earlier project are available in the report entitled *Socio-economic disadvantage and access to higher education*, published by The Policy Press in 2000 (see details at the back of this report).

It should be noted that in the time between these two projects the system by which higher education is funded in Scotland changed. Specifically, from academic year 2000-01 onwards, students in Scotland no longer had to pay their tuition fees in advance, as would be the case under the English system, but had to pay these in arrears (as Graduate Endowment). However, it should be noted that many disadvantaged students, such as those who took part in this project, had previously been means-tested out of paying tuition fees under the old system and so did not gain any benefit from this change. In academic year 2001-02 a further change was introduced to the Scottish system, which provides a 'grant' for some disadvantaged students (the Young Student's Access Bursary). However, only new students are eligible for this payment and so the young people in this research were largely unaffected by this measure. Essentially, this means that the experiences reported by the respondents who took part in this project are likely to more closely resemble those of current students in England than of new students in Scotland.

Glossary

Degree Unlike the rest of the UK, Degree courses at Scottish universities are usually of four years duration. This extra year is known as the **Honours** year. However, students have the option of leaving after only three years with an **Ordinary Degree**. Some, more advanced, Degrees (such as Architecture or Medicine) can last five or more years. Success at Degree level allows access to other **postgraduate** qualifications (such as teacher training, MPhil or PhD)

Highers These are the Scottish exams which perform the same function as **A levels** elsewhere in the UK. That is, they are usually taken in the post-compulsory school years and success in these governs access to **higher education** for school-leavers. These can be studied at a **further education** college by school-leavers, who could be eligible for a local authority bursary.

HNC Higher National Certificate courses involve one year of full-time study and are taught at further education colleges (in England many HNC courses are part-time only). However, like Degrees and HND courses, HNC students do not receive a bursary, but are funded by the system of student loans and tuition fees. Success at HNC can give entry to HND or Degree courses.

HND Higher National Diploma courses last two years full-time, and, as with Degree courses, applications are made in advance through **UCAS** (the Universities and Colleges Admissions Service). However, success at HND level can allow direct access to a Degree course, although the year of entry may vary. It is also possible for some students to leave an HND course after only one year of study with an HNC qualification, or for successful HNC students to enter an HND course directly into the second year of study.

NC The National Certificate is the minimal post-school qualification and school achievement is not a prerequisite for entry. Success at NC level can assist access to HNC level or above. NC is a one-year course full-time. Students at this level in further education are funded by a bursary rather than a system of student loans and tuition fees.

SVQ Scottish Vocational Qualifications and the broader based **GSVQ** (General Scottish Vocational Qualifications) are shorter (modular) courses available at further education colleges and also at secondary schools. Many NC courses incorporate these.

Socioeconomic disadvantage and experience in further and higher education: issues

Introduction

Widening access to, and increasing participation in, further and higher education (FE and HE) are issues that have been a key component of government policy in recent years. Since the late 1980s, participation in higher education in the UK has greatly increased. However, despite this overall expansion, the gap in the level of participation between the most affluent and the most disadvantaged young people has remained clear. There is a definite need to uncover the reasons why this imbalance should have persisted in order to formulate policies capable of redressing this imbalance. The under-representation of less affluent socioeconomic groups in higher education has important implications for social policy, economic efficiency and social justice. These concerns have been highlighted in recent years by the Kennedy, Dearing and Cubie reports. However, it is also the case that this well known problem of the under-representation of less affluent young people in higher education, masks other, less understood, patterns of inequity. These include differences between socioeconomic groups in terms of level of access, institutions attended, types of subjects studied, length of student career, 'drop-out' rates and eventual qualifications gained. Although the relationship between disadvantage and academic success in higher education is unclear and changing, it seems likely that these issues will be mediated by differences in financial support, debt susceptibility, other hardships and group attitudes (cultural perceptions) towards these problems.

In Britain over the past decade, changes in the way in which higher education is funded has

resulted in a shift of the financial burden from the state to the individual student and his or her family. The withdrawal of the universal student maintenance grant, to be replaced by loans (and tuition fees), has placed a number of new financial burdens and fears on both current and potential students. Without appropriate safeguards, it seems likely that young people from disadvantaged family backgrounds will be most negatively affected by the introduction of these measures. For example, such young people may be less willing to take on debt (in the form of student loans), to finance their student career, for both economic and cultural reasons. As we found in the previous report (Forsyth and Furlong, 2000), young people from family backgrounds in which debt seldom exceeds a few pounds may be daunted by the prospect of taking on several thousand pounds worth of loans (in many cases from the outset), with neither guarantee of academic success (and ability to repay) nor any financial safety nets. The problems of student poverty, indebtedness and other hardships (such as poor housing, health, isolation and lack of social life) are likely not only to deter many young people from becoming students in the first place but also to shorten the educational careers of disadvantaged young people who do enter higher education.

Inequities in participation

The above concerns have been highlighted recently by the Cubie Inquiry into student finance, which was commissioned by the Scottish Parliament in the second half of 1999 (Independent Committee of Inquiry into Student Finance, 1999). The committee of inquiry commissioned an exploratory research study into hardship suffered by students from under-represented groups. In this, low-income students were identified as those experiencing the most financial hardship under the contemporary system of student finance. Similarly, a 1999 Department for Education and Employment (DfEE; now the Department for Education and Skills) study by Callender and Kemp (2000) found that students from low social class backgrounds were the most likely to have friends who had been deterred from participation in higher education by perceptions of financial hardship. Both the DfEE and Cubie inquiries uncovered the two key issues to be addressed in this research:

- elevated 'non-completion' rates among disadvantaged students (that is, 'dropping out'); and
- the possibility that many such students complete their careers in full-time education early (that is, leave college or university with a lesser qualification than they had the potential to achieve, because of non-academic reasons related to their disadvantage).

Non-completion ('dropping out')

Anecdotal accounts, such as those described in the reports above, suggest that less affluent students are more likely to drop out of higher education because of financial hardship. This would appear to corroborate figures published in December 1999 by the Scottish Higher Education Funding Council (SHEFC) and the Higher Education Funding Council for England (HEFCE), which showed that education institutions with the highest intakes of less affluent students also had the highest non-completion rates. Such elevated dropout rates are indicative of a high level of wasted resources and carry serious financial implications for funding bodies.

There are several reasons why students from disadvantaged backgrounds may be more likely to drop out of post-compulsory education than their more affluent but similarly qualified peers. These include: cultural isolation, insufficient funds to cover daily living costs, uncontrolled debt, 'missing out' on youthful social activities and financial demands from dependent others. All of these factors are likely to influence a decision to drop out, especially if an alternative (that is, employment) is on offer. Callender and Kemp's (2000) DfEE report found that one in ten

of all full-time students had considered dropping out for financial reasons alone.

These hardships are likely to compound each other and have an impact on the likelihood of academic success. For example, students from disadvantaged backgrounds may be especially reliant on part-time work to fund their way through university or college. This could create time management problems between study and paid work. Any pressure placed on less affluent students, to work longer hours, perhaps in more than one part-time job, or even in full-time employment, in order to finance their studentship, could have a negative impact on coursework. Also, the identity of such individuals may become compromised, between that of 'working student' and that of 'student worker'. These conflicts can only serve to increase the likelihood of a disadvantaged student prematurely terminating his or her course. Any low morale (for example, depression, lack of confidence or loss of ambition) that might result from these hardships and conflicts could only serve to accelerate this process.

Early completion

The rates at which disadvantaged students withdraw from full-time education before achieving their full potential is a more hidden, although perhaps more commonplace, problem than is their elevated dropout rates. For example, compared with their more affluent peers, disadvantaged students who achieve academic success in further education may be less likely to progress to higher education. Similarly, disadvantaged Diplomates may be less likely to progress into Degree courses, disadvantaged Degree students may be less likely to enrol in Honours classes, and disadvantaged Degree graduates may be less likely to apply for a postgraduate qualification. (A full list and short explanation of the all qualifications being studied by respondents in this research is given in the Glossary.)

Early completion, or foregoing the opportunity to progress to a more advanced course, may happen for the same reasons which cause other disadvantaged students to drop out, including poverty, debt and social isolation. In other words, for students from disadvantaged backgrounds a career in post-school education may be limited by the need to compromise between hardship minimisation and their desired level of education. This dilemma is likely to exert the greatest pressure on those who remain in education the longest, either to gain a more advanced qualification (such as an Honours Degree) or because of earlier external disruption to their educational career (for example, illness). Furthermore, these hardships may also influence disadvantaged students' pass rates, grades, subject choices and qualifications. These pressures are likely to be the greatest for those enrolled in lengthy, more prestigious courses (for example, in more highly valued subjects, such as Medicine). In other words, it is the advancement of the most talented disadvantaged students that is most likely to be affected by the hardships detailed above. Again, this is indicative of wasted resources and inequality of opportunity.

Callender and Kemp (2000) found that 78% of students thought that financial pressures deterred students from staying on beyond the minimum amount of time required to gain a basic qualification. Research commissioned by the Cubie Inquiry noted that, as time in education increases, so does accumulated debt. Not only does this have the effect of deterring students from remaining in education for longer than the minimum amount of time, but it also deters others from returning to full-time education after spending time in the workplace. This process, again, appears to be greatest among the most disadvantaged and runs contrary to the present government's policy of 'lifelong learning'. Clearly, there is a need to make returning to education a more appealing prospect to qualified disadvantaged young people in the workplace. Many such young people may only have entered the labour market, as a school-leaver, to satisfy short-term financial needs. Those who do return to full-time education appear likely to be influenced by their experience of this financial security, which may increase their risk of dropping out or early completion.

Research questions

With these issues in mind, this research project asked:

- whether being academically successful at school and being accepted for a course in

higher education are merely the first barriers to career progress encountered by academically talented but disadvantaged young people;
- whether any such barriers increase or decrease in magnitude the longer a disadvantaged young person remains within the education system;
- whether any such barriers are greater or lesser in magnitude for the most talented disadvantaged young people, who access the most prestigious courses;
- why more disadvantaged young people leave higher education either with nothing or with inferior qualifications.

If such processes are found to be at work, this would have serious consequences for the reproduction of inequality and social exclusion, both of which are in no small measure governed by level of education.

Links to the previous project

The barriers faced by disadvantaged young people in accessing further or higher education in the first place were examined in a previous Joseph Rowntree Foundation-funded project, *Socioeconomic disadvantage and access to higher education* (Forsyth and Furlong, 2000). This earlier project explored levels of educational attrition among a disadvantaged school-aged cohort prior to potential entry into higher education; specifically, why some qualified, but disadvantaged, school-leavers fail to take up places in higher education. The previous project confirmed that disadvantaged young people are not enjoying an equal level of participation in higher education as their more advantaged peers. The primary reason for this was the failure of disadvantaged young people to gain sufficient qualifications at school, to allow them access to university. However, it must be emphasised that academic success at school, even within the disadvantaged schools surveyed in this project, was itself a function of social class. Furthermore, it was indicated that disadvantaged young people who *did* gain access to higher education tended to enrol in less prestigious courses, institutions and subjects, as compared to their more advantaged peers. It was also apparent that those few disadvantaged young people who did enter the most prestigious courses were facing the greatest potential barriers to their future advancement, including both cultural and financial difficulties. In this report we will explore how these inequalities develop in later years, by exploring patterns of attrition from within further and higher education among a sample of disadvantaged school-leavers. In other words, this project will assess the impact of student hardship on academic success.

This project builds on the existing sample of disadvantaged young people (*n* = 395) surveyed in the previous project. These young people were recruited in the spring of 1999 from 16 schools located in areas of disadvantage, ranging from inner city to remote highland and island environments. All of the schools selected had below the Scottish national average entry rates to higher education, yet enough pupils in their final year (S6) to allow a viable sample of school-leavers to be recruited. At the start of the current project, all of the respondents in this sample could be described as either full-time students at the start of their careers in higher or further education (first year students) or potential students currently in the labour market (for less than one year). In short, this existing sample of young people from disadvantaged areas displayed a high level of potential involvement with higher education, with over three quarters having already enrolled as full-time students and many of those currently in the labour market intending to do so in the near future.

The findings of this the previous study were strongly indicative of future student hardship. Although the last (100%) quantitative data sweep from that project (a follow-up postal questionnaire) was sent out during only the first week of university term (October 1999), many disadvantaged students in the sample were already expressing concerns about their financial circumstances. This was particularly the case with students who had directly entered higher education, many of whom were already in debt by a four-figured sum to the Student Loans Company. Other concerns raised included the cost of accommodation (particularly from students who were normally resident in study areas remote from institutions of higher education), travel costs and the price of course materials (purchase being necessary at the start of term). For many, these concerns coincided with coming to terms, for the first time, with the daily expenses of independent living. Most

respondents in higher education expected to be in debt to the tune of several thousand pounds by the end of their course, with many expecting that this would take a decade or more to pay off.

Further to these obvious problems, 44 face-to-face qualitative interviews (conducted midway through the students' first year, spring 2000) revealed more subtle deterrent influences on disadvantaged students. These included an unfamiliarity with university culture or student ('middle-class') lifestyle and the pressures of having to forego the youthful social life apparently being enjoyed by both their now employed former peers from their own background and their new more affluent peers at university. At the other end of the spectrum, interviews with some qualified but disadvantaged young people who had entered the labour market on leaving school revealed that they were now preparing to enrol as full-time students at the earliest opportunity. How many of these young people actually do return to full-time education and what additional barriers they encounter are important questions for the current project to address. However, it is the groups endeavouring to continue within full-time higher education who raise the most interesting and policy relevant research issues.

Research methods

This research combines both quantitative and qualitative techniques. The former involved two 100% postal surveys of the 395 participants from the previous research project; the latter involved 81 in-depth face-to-face interviews with a sub-sample of respondents to these surveys. The postal follow-up surveys were primarily intended to 'track' respondents' careers since the previous project. Of these, the final (2001) survey was the most important, as it represented an end point to this research (the students' Degree year). The first (2000) survey was also crucial for sample maintenance, and both surveys were used to select interviewees.

Postal questionnaires were sent out in October 2000 and in October 2001, exactly one and two years after the previous project's postal survey. By comparing their findings, it was possible to chart longitudinally the different educational pathways (trajectories) taken by respondents.

Potentially, these pathways might include respondents who:

- had dropped out;
- had completed a course and consequently completed their career in education;
- had completed a course and then progressed to another (more advanced) course;
- had to repeat (a year of study in) the same course;
- had changed their course (institution, qualification or subject) entirely;
- had returned to education after having discontinued a previous course;
- had only enrolled in full-time education after spending time in the labour market;
- had 'successfully' advanced straight from school to their Degree (that is, third) year at university by the end of the project.

In this way it was hoped to identify whether the most disadvantaged students had more difficult or complicated career pathways, with fewer respondents passing along the straight to Degree route, as compared with their more affluent peers.

The qualitative interviews were conducted during the spring of 2001 and 2002. These interviews were designed to unravel why students from disadvantaged backgrounds had moved along each of the various educational pathways uncovered in the quantitative phase described above. Interviewees were selected from the postal questionnaire data in order to cover as wide a variety of educational pathways as possible. It was hoped thus to identify the underlying reasons for why some disadvantaged students fair particularly poorly within higher education.

Summary

The main aim of this project is to identify ways by which the success rate in higher education of qualified but disadvantaged school-leavers can be improved. Despite much anecdotal evidence, the relationship between student hardship and dropout rates is unclear. This project measures the impact of financial, geographical, cultural and other barriers on the success rate of disadvantaged students. With the full impact of recent changes to the system of funding higher education still to be felt, this project is at the centre of current debates concerning how higher education can be made more accessible to young people from disadvantaged backgrounds. There is clear evidence that lack of education plays a key role in the reproduction of disadvantage. It is therefore essential to identify ways in which participation in higher education can not only be broadened but also made more equitable. By drawing attention to the factors, or barriers, which discourage continued participation within higher education, this project aims to identify how effective policies might be developed to redress these inequalities. The next chapter begins this process by detailing the patterns of underlying disadvantage of the respondents who took part in this research.

Destinations of disadvantaged school-leavers

Introduction

This chapter quantifies patterns of attrition among disadvantaged school-leavers entering further and higher education. This is done by examining the sample recruited in the previous project in order to use it as a 'baseline' from which to measure any later transitions within full-time education. This chapter also describes how the research sample was derived, as well as detailing respondents' demographic backgrounds (levels of disadvantage) and prior educational attainment.

Sample selection and recruitment

The baseline sample consisted of 395 young people who completed their final year of secondary school (S6) in the summer of 1999. These young people were recruited from 16 schools, all of which had entrance rates to higher education below the Scottish national average. These entrance rates were a reflection of the schools' catchment areas, each being situated in an area of disadvantage. The schools, and hence the young people who participated in the project, were located in four distinct geographical 'study areas'. These were Glasgow City (seven schools), North Lanarkshire (three schools), Ayrshire (four schools) and rural Argyll (two schools). The numbers of schools in each study area is a reflection of anticipated numbers of young people enrolling in higher education, as calculated from entrance rates and school size. Each of the four study areas was chosen to represent environments displaying different types of socioeconomic disadvantage in relation to accessing higher education. The Glasgow study area schools were selected to recruit qualified, but disadvantaged, young people from a 'deprived' inner-city environment. Despite containing the majority of the most deprived postcodes in Scotland, this city holds a broad range of educational institutions, including three universities. The Lanarkshire schools were located within a conurbation of large industrial towns. This study area has no universities, but is within easy commuting distance to Glasgow. The Ayrshire schools were located in small ex-industrial towns with semi-rural catchment areas. This county also has no universities based within its boundaries, although the nearby town of Ayr contains two higher education campuses. Commuting to Glasgow is possible for most young people living in these small towns, but this is much more difficult than from Lanarkshire. Finally, both the Argyll schools had remote highland and island catchment areas. At the time of recruitment, there were no post-school educational institutions based in this county. This study area is relatively more affluent than the other three, but this relative affluence is offset by the fact that, for all respondents in this sub-sample, enrolment in higher education necessitated moving home. Thus, recruitment locations for this project ranged between multiply-deprived inner-city neighbourhoods within walking distance of higher education institutions, through large towns near to such institutions, to small towns more distant from post-school education provision, to remote rural areas with no such provision.

The baseline sample

In the previous research project, data were collected from the 395 participants in two separate data sweeps. Together, these datasets are hereafter termed as the 'baseline data' in the current research project. This baseline data comprises background information (for example, basic demographics) collected during the spring of 1999, while respondents were still in their final school year, and information on school-leaver destinations (for example, student characteristics) collected by postal questionnaire the following October. The baseline postal survey was conducted at a time when all of those who did access higher education would be at the beginning of their career at university. The mean ages of respondents at the times of data collection were 17.0 and 17.6 years old respectively. Comparing these two earlier datasets revealed which respondents were able to directly access higher education and which were not. Full details of the baseline sample's demographics are shown in Appendix A.

Disadvantage and prior educational attainment

The majority of respondents in the baseline sample was female (60%). This is in part a function of fewer males 'staying on' at school in areas of disadvantage (see the previous report for details).[1] Nearly three quarters (73%) of respondents lived in relatively deprived postcode areas (as defined by the Carstairs and Morris (1991) DEPCAT system,[2] that is >4). This is as might be expected given the characteristics of the geographical localities in which respondents were recruited. However, only around half of respondents (50%) could be described as 'working class' (that is, manual class), as defined by the Registrar General's occupational classification system, according to their parents' occupations. This figure excludes 51 respondents (13%) who could not provide a parental occupation for classification. This

happened for a variety of reasons, including parents who were (always) unemployed, sick, disabled, in education, institutionalised or full-time caregivers, with respondents often being unaware of an absent parent's occupation (even if they were working).

This social class distribution suggests that many of those who access higher education from deprived localities are atypical of their communities, having come from the more affluent local families. This phenomenon works to the benefit of the current research project, as it provides a *relatively* advantaged sub-group (44% of the total sample) which can act as a comparison group to the *more* disadvantaged young people in the sample. However, it must be stressed that this 'control' group's 'affluence' is only relative, and in no way can these any of respondents be described as an elite (only 25 respondents were in social class I). The most common parental occupations among this *relatively* advantaged group were, in social class II, primary school teacher ($n = 23$) and, in social class IIIN, sales assistant ($n = 34$). Although, many of these were previous occupations or those of single parents, it is nevertheless clear that the parental occupational class of the baseline sample was, on the whole, above what might have been expected given the catchment areas of the schools in which it was recruited. This seems likely to be a function of a greater attrition rate among disadvantaged young people operating within these schools.

School achievement

The process of excess educational attrition among the disadvantaged can be illustrated by comparing school achievement in the baseline sample across the social classes. In Scotland, Highers exams play a similar role to A levels, elsewhere in the UK, in determining whether academic achievement is of a sufficient standard to gain entry to a course in higher education. At the time of this research, Highers exams were first taken in school year S5 (the penultimate year), with more Highers (either 're-sits' or additional ones) often being taken in S6 (the final year). This is different from the system elsewhere in the UK where A level exams are normally sat at the end of the final school year (although the new AS level system is more like that of Highers). The simplest way to represent

---

[1] According to the Scottish Executive, in 2001, approximately 10% more females than males remained in school beyond the minimum leaving age, with around 31% of Scottish females, aged 16 to 21 years, enrolling in higher education, compared with only 25% of Scottish males.

[2] This Carstairs and Morris DEPCAT system uses levels of male unemployment, overcrowding, low social class and car ownership to classify every postcode sector in Scotland on a seven-point scale from DEPCAT 1 (most affluent) to DEPCAT 7 (most deprived).

academic success at school among this population is by using the Highers 'points' system. This awards points to each grade of Higher as follows: grade 'A' six points, 'B' four points, 'C' two points and 'D' one point. The mean points score for the whole baseline sample was 11.8, after both years (S5 and S6) of examinations. This ranged between the 49 (12%) respondents who left school with no points at all, to one respondent who left with 48 points. These final points totals are slightly misleading, as, having already gained sufficient Highers points to access university in S5, many of the most successful pupils studied other courses in S6 (such as a Certificate of Sixth Year Studies).

In S5 a maximum of five Highers may be taken. From these S5 results, there were only seven 'straight A' pupils in the sample, with 81 (22%) respondents gaining no points at this stage. The mean Highers points score at this time was only 7.5. To put this into context, at some universities (such as the University of Glasgow), the minimum level of achievement to secure entrance is considered as roughly 12 points or better (that is, three 'B's), although this rule varies by subject and institution, according to popularity and prestige. By this yardstick, only 27% of the baseline sample had attained this level of academic achievement in S5, rising to 45% after S6. Clearly, many respondents relied on their S6 Highers results to gain access to higher education, rather than the more direct route of securing a place prior to leaving school from S5

results alone, allowing pupils time to prepare for university study (in Certificate of Sixth Year Studies classes). Figure 1 shows the distribution of Highers points across respondents' social class, broken down by the final total of points and those gained at the first attempt (in S5).

Figure 1, shows a strong social class gradient in academic success at school. From this it is clear that 'middle class' respondents were more successful in gaining the qualifications required to access higher education, both from the initial S5 results *and* from further Highers examinations sat in S6. Also shown, as column 'X', on this figure are the 51 respondents who could not be allocated to a social class. This group had the lowest mean Highers points score. This is not surprising, as in many ways this group can be considered the most disadvantaged in the sample.

As level of school achievement governs level of access to post-school education, the above findings had implications for the future destinations of respondents. In order to see which respondents were more likely to be successful at gaining Highers points, an inferential statistical analysis was conducted. This was a multiple linear regression correlation analysis, which used all the demographic variables (measures of disadvantage, listed in Appendix A, collected while respondents were still at school, prior to their final round of examinations) to predict their final Highers points total (the dependent variable). Four such variables were found to be predictive of academic success at school. These were:

- living in the remote (Argyll) study area;
- having family members who had been in post-school education
- the variables measuring parental social class;
- respondents who could not be 'classified' or allocated to a social class.

In other words, the distribution of academic success could be predicted by social class, with the *relatively* more affluent young people gaining superior qualifications within (the same disadvantaged) school as their more disadvantaged peers. This confirms the hypothesis that educational attrition is greatest among the disadvantaged while at school. However, as we will see in later sections, this measure of school achievement (itself governed

Figure 1: Social class and school achievement

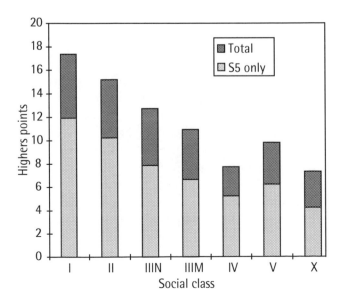

by levels of advantage), is also strongly predictive of post-school educational pathways.[3]

Disadvantage and access to post-school education

At baseline, the respondents who took part in this research had arrived at a broad range of school-leaver destinations; however, around three quarters (76%) became full-time students. Most of these had enrolled in Degree courses (n = 170); other courses enrolled in included HND (n = 47), HNC (n = 26) and NC (n = 47).[4] The remaining quarter (24%) of respondents had left full-time education and entered a variety of labour market destinations, including full-time employment (n = 51), part-time work only (n = 8), government training schemes such as 'skill-seekers' (n = 14) and unemployment (n = 17). One respondent had returned to secondary school. Of these 'non-students', around one third (32%) stated that they would *not* be applying for entry to post-school education in the following year, with around another third (35%) stating that they had already done so; the remaining third being undecided. Therefore, it appeared that many of those who had not gone straight from school to university or college could better be described as 'deferrers' rather than 'rejecters' of post-school education.

As might be expected, levels of access to higher education varied by social class. This is because level of access was governed by prior school achievement, which was, in turn, a function of social class (see Figure 2).

The importance of Highers points in dictating level of access to post-school education was confirmed by a similar statistical procedure to that undertaken to predict Highers points (see Appendix B, Regression 2). This indicated that

prior school achievement (Highers points) was strongly predictive of the level of access on the four-level continuum (shown in Figure 2), between Degree (that is, courses of three or more years duration), HND (two-year courses), HNC or further education (one-year or shorter courses), and not being in post-school education. Of all demographic variables, only being from a more deprived postcode (DEPCAT) was still in the equation predicting level of access, when controlling for Highers points. In other words, the effect of social class on level of access is as a result of pre-existing qualifications (although these are themselves a function of disadvantage). It should be remembered that this only refers to initial level of access to post-school education and not eventual outcome (for example, qualifications obtained). It is possible that some respondents not in education at this stage may be taking a 'year out' before entering post-school education, for example. Nevertheless, this indicates that the *relatively* affluent young people within the sample were more likely to enrol in Degree courses directly after leaving school, as compared with all other destinations. In contrast the *most* disadvantaged young people in the sample appeared more likely to enter non-Degree courses.

---

[3] Full details of this regression analysis, Regression 1, and all other such analyses conducted in this research are shown in Appendix B.

[4] It must be stressed again that even those who enrolled in non-Degree courses in this sample are atypical of young people living in their local communities, most of whom did not even remain in school until the final year (S6) when recruitment for this research took place.

Figure 2: Social class and initial level of access to post-school education

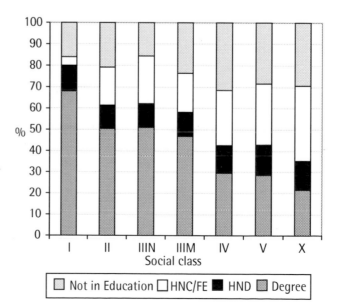

Summary

In this chapter we have described a baseline sample of disadvantaged young people, whose paths through post-school education are tracked in subsequent data sweeps. At this stage it was apparent that the *relatively* advantaged young people within the sample were able to access post-school education at a more advanced level from the outset. This was mainly a function of their better school qualifications. These findings raise a number of important questions concerning the future educational pathways which respondents may take from their different starting positions (baseline). For example, would those in further education progress to higher education? Would those who entered the labour market return to full-time education? And how many full-time students would drop out of or complete their careers in post-school education at an early stage? Specifically, would these pathways work in favour of, or against, the most disadvantaged young people? In other words, would the pattern of inequity detailed in this chapter persist, diminish or become stronger with experience in further and higher education? In the next chapter we begin detailing the research that was undertaken to address these important questions.

Patterns of participation in further and higher education

Introduction

This chapter follows the progress of the baseline sample of disadvantaged school-leavers recruited in low achieving schools located in areas of deprivation, as detailed in the previous chapter. In order to do this, two postal follow-up surveys were conducted, timed to collect data exactly one and two years after the baseline postal survey was conducted. At the end of this procedure respondents who had left school and directly enrolled in higher education should (in theory) be at the beginning of their Degree (third) year. Those who had enrolled in further education should by now have finished that course and (perhaps) have progressed to higher education. However, other respondents may have left full-time education, while others still may have only recently enrolled for the first time. This chapter describes patterns of educational attainment and the procedures used to measure these over the duration of this project. How the young people who took part in this research differed from the wider student population is also described in this chapter.

'Interim' follow-up survey

In October 2000 a postal questionnaire was sent out to all 395 respondents. At this point all respondents were either 18 or 19 years of age (mean 18.6). A number of difficulties in contacting respondents were encountered using this procedure. These included respondents having left their parental home, having moved between temporary addresses (for example, within student accommodation) and, in particular, having changed their permanent (that is, parental) address. The wholesale slum

clearance of housing 'schemes' in the East End of Glasgow, where much of the city study area sub-sample had been recruited, presented a particular impediment. Despite these difficulties and the time elapsed since the previous study, 319 of the young people responded on this occasion. This response rate (of 81%) was much higher than anticipated and perhaps reflects a high level of concern among young people about the issues being addressed by this research. As well as keeping track of each respondent's progress, this survey also functioned as a sample maintenance measure, by keeping in contact with participants to ensure a good response rate for the final (and most important) survey, which was conducted during the following year.

'Final' follow-up survey

In October 2001, another postal questionnaire was sent out to all 395 baseline respondents. By this time, all respondents were either 19 or 20 years of age (mean 19.6). This data sweep was intended to be the final survey, as it was timed to coincide with the point when the most successful students should have entered their Degree year at university. On this occasion 308 (78%) completed questionnaires were returned. It should be noted that this 308 was not a sub-set of the interim survey's 319 respondents. In fact, 40 respondents who had responded in 2000 did not do so in 2001, while 29 who did not respond to the interim survey did so on this occasion. This means that responses rates varied between the 279 (71%) who responded to both surveys, and the 348 (88%) who responded to either. It was decided to use the 308 who had responded to the 2001 postal survey as the final sample in all future analyses, as it was possible to retrospectively reconstruct their status in October

2000 from their responses in this final questionnaire.

Sample attrition

It had been anticipated that those who failed to participate in the final sample would be more likely to be among the most disadvantaged of baseline respondents. This was, in part, because of the greater difficulty in reaching these young people (for example, due to urban redevelopment) and also because of the likelihood of a greater level of continued attrition from education among the most disadvantaged young people. Indeed, respondents who lived in the most deprived postcodes were less likely to have participated (ranging between 87% in DEPCAT 4 and 63% in DEPCAT 7). Between the four study areas, inner city Glasgow respondents were the least likely to have participated (68%), those from remote Argyll were the most likely (87%). Interestingly, despite this, there was no significant difference in response rate between respondents from Social Inclusion Partnership (SIP) and non-SIP areas. The differences in response rates across DEPCAT areas may be, at least in part, due to geographical factors (such as the slum clearance in Glasgow), because Glasgow respondents were mainly resident in DEPCATs 6 and 7 (85%), while Argyll respondents parental home addresses were mainly in DEPCAT 4 (75%).

Baseline respondents in social classes IV or V also appeared less likely to respond (67 and 62% respectively). However, there was no significant difference in response rate between manual and non-manual classes combined, nor was there between 'unclassified' respondents and those who could be allocated to a parental social class. As might be expected, non-participants in the final sample had a poorer level of school achievement than participants (mean Highers points 8.4 and 12.9 respectively). As it was known that social class was correlated with school achievement, and hence access to higher education, a more sophisticated analysis was conducted to see which factors predicted (non-) participation (see Appendix B, Regression 3). This analysis found that Highers points was the best predictor of continued participation in this research, along with being from a less deprived postcode (DEPCAT) and the small town study area (Ayrshire). This implies that any social class

differences in participation rates could be accounted for by area of residence and, in particular, (poor) school achievement. In other words, those who did not participate tended to be less well qualified. (Further details of the final sample demographics and how these compare with the baseline sample can be seen in Appendices A and C.)

Students and non-students

By the time of the final follow-up survey, more than one third (36%) of respondents were no longer in full-time education. The 110 non-students in the final survey included 78 respondents who were in full-time employment, 14 who were only in part-time employment, three in government training schemes and six who were unemployed. On this occasion, most non-students (n = 66) stated that they did not expect to be in full-time education in the following year. However, 16 were currently applying for a full-time studentship, two were attempting to 'get back in' to a course from which they had been suspended and four were applying for part-time study only. Also, 19 'non-students' were currently studying part-time, including two engaged in Degree, one in HND and five in HNC courses. Eight individuals were currently engaged in Modern Apprenticeships.

Most of the 198 full-time students in the final sample were studying for a Degree. In fact, these 153 individuals constituted almost half the entire sample (50%). The remaining 45 'current' students were enrolled in a variety of other courses including 32 HND students, 19 HNC and, on this occasion, only one NC. This range of courses is quite different from that at the baseline because, by the time of the final survey, all respondents who initially enrolled in non-Degree courses should have completed these (apart from some longer Nursing courses, n = 9). The demographic background of students in the sample reflected that of the baseline sample in that most (64%) were female, most were from areas of disadvantage (65% in DEPCAT 5-7), yet many were *relatively* advantaged (only 42% of current students, that could be 'classified', were in a manual social class). The social class gradient, in terms of level of participation in education, among the final 308 participants, was

Figure 3: Social class and 'final' destination

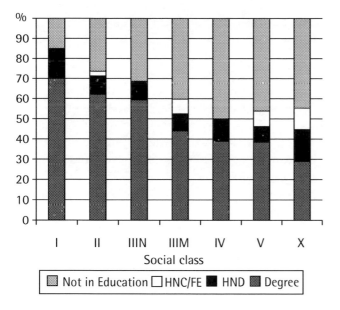

Legend: Not in Education / HNC/FE / HND / Degree

Institutions attended

The patterns of courses enrolled in and subjects studied by respondents were reflected in the types of institutions they attended. As the majority of all students were studying Degree courses at universities, these institutions were subdivided into three categories according to the three phases of university development in the UK. These three types of HE institution will be termed as 'ivy league', 'red brick' and 'new' universities in this research. 'Ivy league' in the Scottish context refers to ancient universities who received their charters several hundred years ago. Such institutions are usually regarded as the most prestigious and tend to offer the most advanced courses or subjects. Examples of such institutions include Glasgow (University), Edinburgh and St Andrew's. 'Red brick' is defined here as universities established during the 20th century prior to 1990. These are either located in major cities, often specialising in courses which reflect the local industrial heritage, or are located on purpose-built campuses. Examples of these include Strathclyde (in Glasgow), Heriot-Watt (in Edinburgh) and Stirling. 'New' universities refer to the former polytechnic colleges, which were awarded their charters during the expansion of higher education that occurred throughout the UK during the 1990s. Examples include, Caledonian (in Glasgow), Napier (in Edinburgh) and Paisley. Such universities often have the highest numbers of non-standard students (for example, those of low social class, mature students and those from ethnic minority groups), as well as the highest dropout rates. Table 1 shows the number of respondents attending each type of institution and what they were studying at the time of the final survey. (A full list of all the institutions attended by respondents is given in Appendix E.)

found to have persisted to this stage. This is shown by Figure 3.

As might be expected, it is apparent from Figure 3 that, more than two years after leaving school, relatively few respondents were still enrolled in courses of less than three years duration (that is, non-Degree courses). At this stage however, it is worth remembering that some Degree courses last longer than three years. Specifically, some advanced or prestigious Degrees, in subjects such as Medicine, are only awarded after courses lasting five or more years. At the other end of the scale, many subjects, such as Nursing, are available in variety of course lengths (such as HNC, HND or Degree). Relatively few respondents in this research were enrolled in the more prestigious or advanced Degree courses. For example, by the time of final data sweep only four (2%) respondents were enrolled in the SHEFC subject group 'Medicine, Veterinary Medicine and Dentistry', while 36 (18%) were enrolled in subjects grouped by SHEFC as 'Health and Welfare'. This compares figures for all Scottish students in these respective SHEFC subject groups of 5,881 (5%) and 9,759 (8%) during session 1999-2000 (when most respondents chose their subjects). This raises the question of whether this disparity is solely due to underachievement or whether it has also been shaped by other factors that influence course choice? (A full list of subjects studied by respondents at the time of each data sweep is given in Appendix D.)

From Table 1, it can be seen that most HND students in the sample were studying at FE colleges. The largest number of Degree students were enrolled at 'red brick' universities, although the total number (Degree plus HND) enrolled at 'new' universities was similar. 'Ivy league' universities appeared relatively less well attended in this sample, as did other institutions of higher education (for example art school or agricultural college). What is not revealed in Table 1 is the geographical locations of these institutions, in particular, that respondents tended to be at institutions closest to their parental home. This

Table 1: Types of institution attend and course studied by respondents (*n* = 308)

	Degree	HND	HNC/FE course
'Ivy league' university	38	0	0
'Red brick' university	59	1	0
'New' university	46	10	0
HE college	5	0	0
FE college	5	21	13
Total	153	32	13

was even the case with the remote Argyll students – all bar one of whom (a remote learner) had left their parental home in order to access post-school education. As a consequence of this, more than two thirds of university students attended one of three Glasgow-based institutions.

Choices of university

The three Glasgow-based universities represent a microcosm of university provision in the UK. They comprise one 'ivy league' institution (the University of Glasgow) one 'red brick' (Strathclyde University) and one 'new' (Glasgow Caledonian University). Using a range of academic indicators, *The Sunday Times* publication, *The good university guide 2001*, ranked Glasgow 20th, Strathclyde 39th and Caledonian 72nd of the UK's 97 universities. The rank order of these universities in terms of entrants from state schools is the reverse of this. In 1999 (the year most respondents enrolled in university) Caledonian was ranked 4th, Strathclyde 31st and Glasgow 67th. Dropout rates between types of institution reflect these access figures. In 2001 Caledonian had the joint highest dropout rank in the UK; Strathclyde was ranked joint 23rd and Glasgow joint 43rd. In other words, institutions with higher numbers of less affluent students had lower success rates.

In theory, the three Glasgow-based universities should be equally geographically accessible to respondents (although the University of Glasgow is located in the city's 'West End' student residential area; the other two are in the city centre). In reality, only 38 respondents had *ever* attended Glasgow University, compared with 48 at Strathclyde and 47 at Caledonian. The relative

numbers of respondents who accessed each of these three institutions are interesting in that the 'ivy league' institution had the fewest respondents in attendance in both absolute and relative terms. This was despite Glasgow being both the largest institution and the one that receives the most applications. For example, according to UCAS figures, in 2000, Glasgow received 3,892 new entrants through UCAS applications from within the UK. The corresponding figures for Strathclyde and Glasgow Caledonian were 3,136 and 3,163 respectively. This begs the question of whether a disproportionate number of student respondents are discouraged from applying to the more prestigious 'ivy league' institution, or whether these figures are merely because they could not gain access due to their lower school achievement (Glasgow's average Higher entrance points was 24.2, compared with only 19.8 for Strathclyde and 14.9 for Glasgow Caledonian).

Not only was Glasgow University less well attended than its rivals within the city, but enrolment at other 'ivy league' institutions was rare in this research. By the time of the final survey, when 34 respondents were still attending Glasgow University, only four respondents were enrolled at any other 'ivy league' university. This compares with 17 respondents who were attending 'red brick' and 27 who were attending 'new' universities outside the city. At this time 42 respondents were attending Strathclyde and 30 were (still) attending Glasgow Caledonian – an almost a 1:1 ratio with other 'new' universities. Furthermore, most non-Glasgow-based university students attended institutions within commuting distance of Glasgow (Stirling, *n* = 10, Paisley, *n* = 17 and Edinburgh-based institutions, *n* = 8). In contrast, only four respondents had *ever* attended any university outside Scotland (all 'new' universities in England). Nearly two thirds (65%) of all students stated that they currently attended the institution nearest to their parental home that offered the course they were studying. Clearly there is reluctance among these respondents to attend institutions outside the west of Scotland. This limits the range of institutions that they can attend, in particular, courses at prestigious institutions. This raises the question of whether these young peoples' reluctance to move is as a result of deep-seated cultural factors or is simply due to the financial costs involved with moving house and independent living.

Student lifestyle and finance

Travel and accommodation

At the time of the final survey more than half (60%) of students were still living with their parents. This figure rises to almost three quarters (74%) when the remote Argyll students are excluded (the corresponding figure for non-students was 92%). To put this into a national context, the DfEE survey of UK students by Callender and Kemp (2000) estimated that, by their second year of study, only around 17% of students are still living with their parents. Of the students in this research who had left their parental home by the time of the final survey, 12 were living in halls of residence, 30 in student-only let flats, 28 were renting in the private sector, five were owner occupiers and five were council house tenants. The advantages of 'moving out' are obvious. Not only does it increase the choice of institutions open to the potential student, but it also makes it easier to enjoy a greater level of participation in student life (such as library access and social networking). Despite this, it was obvious from their addresses that many respondents in this research who had left their parental home were not currently resident in stereotypically 'student areas' (only 10 students had moved to the West End of Glasgow).

Another way in which leaving home benefits the student is that it minimises travel time. Students who had chosen to remain in their parental home were often incurring substantial travel costs, both in terms of time and money. The mean daily travel time among stay-at-home students was 1 hour, 41 minutes, compared with only 42 minutes among those who had left home. Although remaining in the parental home may be viewed as a cost-minimising strategy, clearly much of this saving may be offset by greater expenditure on travel.

Expenditure

Travel and accommodation were only two of a number of costs incurred by students in this project. Table 2 compares the different sources of expenditure for students and non-students at the time the final survey.

From Table 2, it can be seen that total weekly expenditure between students and non-students was remarkably similar (£94 and £90.73 respectively). However, students and non-students tended to be spending this sum on different things. For example, compared with non-students, significantly more students were incurring travel expenses. Interestingly, although significantly fewer students were paying towards their accommodation, the students who did incur this cost tended to being paying significantly more. This implies that students still living with their parents were less likely to be paying any 'dig money', as compared with their non-student peers, while students who had left the parental

Table 2: Weekly expenditure of students and non-students compared

	Students		Non-students	
Expenditure source	% incurring cost	Mean incurred	% incurring cost	Mean incurred
Travel (eg fares and petrol)	93	£15.90	82**	£17.56
Accommodation	55	£40.53	71**	£29.01##
Bills (eg mobile phone)	63	£9.33	54	£16.25###
Groceries and clothing	87	£21.82	74**	£23.38
Luxury and consumer goods	70	£9.79	66	£11.64
Alcohol, tobacco, 'etc'	64	£17.02	68	£24.02#
Other social life costs	67	£14.16	67	£19.80##
Books and work materials	81	£6.28	11***	£5.48
Other (eg driving lessons)	4	£14.00	11*	£22.50
Total	n = 198	£94.00	n = 110	£90.73

Notes: Significant differences between students and non-students in terms of numbers incurring * $p < 0.05$, ** $p < 0.01$ and *** $p < 0.001$ (by chi-square) and between students and non-students in terms of amount spent by those incurring # $p < 0.05$, ## $p < 0.01$ and ### $p < 0.001$ (by 2-tailed T-Test).

home were facing much higher accommodation costs. Overall, students appeared to be facing a greater range of financial needs (at least in terms of books). This may explain why students spent less on paying bills and on socialising, despite being equally as likely to incur these costs as non-students. The popular stereotype of a 'party animal' social life was not supported by the pattern of expenditure of the students who took part in this research (although this may be more applicable to more affluent students).

Income

What Table 2 does not take account of is the underlying spending power of the students and non-students in the final sample. This is shown in Table 3, which details various sources of income on which respondents were able to draw.

Two things are apparent from Table 3. First, non-students had a greater overall income. In fact, on average, non-student income considerably exceeded their stated expenditure (by £46.77 per week), while average student income was little more than their expenditure (£4.67), with many (43%) students actually recording a net deficit (two had equal income and expenses). Second, students' and non-students' income sources differed greatly. Unlike students, most of the non-students derived all their income from only one source, namely paid work. Although two thirds (66%) of students also had income from work, this was much less than that earned by the non-students. The other major source of income for students in this sample was loans. Owing to recent changes in

the way that higher education is funded, it is difficult to compare these figures with other student surveys, other than in terms of the proportions in receipt of each income source. For example, Callender and Kemp (2000) (also) found that 72% of full-time students had taken out a loan. However, at the time of their research, 64% of students were in receipt of the, now abolished, maintenance grant; 88% received income from their family; 62% had worked during the academic year. With a much heavier reliance on loans, students in the current research project are clearly more at risk of going into debt.

Student debt

Of the 198 respondents currently in full-time education, 154 (78%) stated that they were already in debt. The mean current amount owed by *all* current students was £5,902, rising to £6,596 among those who were in debt (range £150-£15,000). This compares with figures from the DfEE survey (Callender and Kemp, 2000), which gave an average debt for *all* full-time students of only £2,528. Student loans accounted for most of respondents' debts in this research and these had been taken out by 143 current students (mean £5,858, range £200-£13,000). However, 83 respondents (42% of all students) were currently (also) in *other* debt (mean £773, range £100-£10,000). Some students had up to four sources of 'other' debt, including bank overdrafts (*n* = 59) and credit cards (*n* = 21). Levels of debt were greatest among those who had attained the most academically. Only 18 of the 114 third-year Degree students in the sample were not in debt. The mean total already owed

Table 3: Weekly income of students and non-students compared

Income source	Students		Non-students	
	% in receipt	Mean received	% in receipt	Mean received
Parents/Family	41	£31.19	15***	£28.64
Work	66	£60.14	89***	£149.91###
Bursaries	15	£74.71	0	–
Loans	72	£50.56	0	–
Other (eg scholarships, benefit)	15	£24.37	11	£32.35
Total	*n* = 198	£98.68	*n* = 110	£137.50###

Notes: Significant differences between students and non-students in terms numbers in receipt * $p < 0.05$, ** $p < 0.01$ and *** $p < 0.001$ (by chi-square) and between students and non-students in terms of amount received by those in receipt # $p < 0.05$, ## $p < 0.01$ and ### $p < 0.001$ (by 2-tailed T-Test).

by these students was £6,300 (£7,506 among debtors only). It must be stressed that these figures are an underestimate of the debt that many of these students will end up with. For example, 16 of 44 students who claimed not to be in debt stated that they were in receipt of income from student loans (presumably these had not yet arrived or had not yet been spent), while some, such as those in receipt of scholarships, had taken out a loan and invested this as a safeguard against future hardship (such as unemployment after graduation). Also, many Degree students will be taking out more loans in the future, should they decided to enrol in an Honours year or if they are studying for Degrees in lengthy, more prestigious subjects.

Student employment

One way in which students can pay off or minimise their debt is to take on part-time work. Only 13 students in the final survey had *never* been employed since becoming a student, most of whom (*n* = 8) had only just enrolled in the first year of their course during the previous month. Forty respondents had only worked outside term time ('summer jobs'), 62 had only worked during term time and the remaining 79 had worked both. A majority (63%) of current students was employed at the time of the final survey (during term time). These respondents were working a mean of 14.7 hours per week (range 2.5-35 hours). The Cubie Inquiry into student finance recommended that no student should work more than 10 hours maximum per week during term time. By this measure, 64% of working students were exceeding this maximum limit (three were working a 35-hour week). (It should be noted that these figures are likely to be an underestimate, as many respondents may not have found work at the start of their academic year, when funds have just arrived, and, as will be detailed later, many respondents cut back on their working hours during their latter years of study.) Two thirds of working students (67%) stated that their job did not (currently) clash with their study time (that is, classes), however, less than half (45%) stated that their job did not tire them out when trying to studying. This may be in part because many students also had to travel to their place of work. Some working students were fortunate enough to live and work in the same areas as their

institution (26% in their parental home and 23% at term-time addresses). Others commuted to their institution, while retaining jobs in their home area (28%), and others still were involved in more complicated commuting patterns, including travelling *from* their term-time address back *to* their home area (6%). Nearly one quarter (23%) were still in the same job that they had when they were at school. Only 13 respondents had course-related employment; other student jobs included shop assistants (*n* = 44), table waiting (*n* = 13), bar work (*n* = 12), call-centre telesales and 'fast food' (both *n* = 9). Eleven respondents currently had two jobs.

These findings are comparable to those of a study by Barke et al (2000) for the DfEE, which involved 879 students attending a 'new' university (with a high proportion of local 'working class' students). In that study levels of term-time employment were lower, perhaps reflecting lower levels of disadvantage in their sample. However, the pattern of student employment among those who were working was very similar to that found in this project. Such students were more likely to still be living with their parents, working a mean of 14.2 hours per week, most often as sales assistants, in catering or in telesales. These students felt that taking on paid employment had a negative impact on their academic performance and those who were in term-time jobs were found to be faring less well in their examinations. As with this project, the most disadvantaged students in Barke et al's research were those who were the most averse to taking on debt. All of these are themes that will be explored in greater detail in the later chapters of this report.

Summary

More than two years after leaving school, around two thirds of respondents were still involved in education, either as full-time students, as part-time students or as applicants for the following year. Despite their high rate of involvement in post-school education, in several ways these young people appeared to differ from the wider student population. First, they appeared to be much less likely to have left their parental home than other students of their age. Second, and related to this, they appeared to have a strong tendency to enrol at their most local institutions (even among those who had made a housing transition). Third, this may have in turn have contributed to them being much less likely to enrol at more prestigious institutions. Fourth, and perhaps related to institution choice, respondents appear to have chosen less advanced courses or subjects, which could perhaps be described as vocational, offering sort-term economic gain rather than cultural capital. It is possible that their relative disadvantages may have influenced respondents' choices. For example, not being able to afford to leave home limits choice of institution. In this sample, enrolment in prestigious courses at institutions other than the local University of Glasgow, was particularly limited.

At this stage, many students in this research were already in a great deal of debt, with few receiving non-repayable bursaries and less than half receiving any contribution from their parents. Paid work, often during term time, appeared to be the main alternative to student debt. Those averse to debt clearly risked eating into their study time by taking on (more) paid work. Whether issues relating to this stark choice between debt and paid work lead to reduced participation, such as early completion or dropping out of full-time education, will be explored in later chapters. Another possibility is that many of the respondents in this research who chose (or switched to) a shorter, more vocational course, perhaps with a set career path on graduation, may have done so to maximise the likelihood of swiftly settling their student debt. Such complicated student career trajectories will be explored in greater detail in the following chapter.

Patterns of success in further and higher education

Introduction

This chapter quantifies the educational pathways taken by the disadvantaged school-leavers who took part in this research and, in so doing, identifies any factors relating to their pre-existing disadvantage that may have acted as barriers to their continued academic success. This is done by comparing the educational attainment of the respondents who participated in the final postal survey, detailed in the previous chapter, with their level of attainment at the time of the baseline survey, detailed in Chapter 2. The final survey's questionnaire was designed to be directly comparable to that used in the baseline survey in order to measure any changes in level of participation in higher education that may have occurred over the duration of the project. Statistical analyses were then conducted in order to see whether any changes made to level of participation in post-school education between the surveys could be predicted from the data collected at the start of the project. In other words, this chapter predicts which academically talented young people are likely to be successful in higher education and which are not.

Career pathways of disadvantaged students

Continuing students

At this stage it is worth remembering that the participation rates in higher education detailed in the previous chapter principally referred to where these young people were at the time of the final follow-up survey. Although a majority (55%) of respondents had been in full-time education

throughout the duration of this project, many respondents had changed their career paths during this time. Specifically, some respondents had only started their career in higher education during this time, while others had discontinued (dropped out or completed). Others had remained in full-time education, but had changed their level of participation (course or institution). It was even possible for respondents to have changed their career paths more than once. For example, one respondent had enrolled in three separate courses (at the time of each survey). Clearly, the potential range of changing educational pathways along which the respondents in this research could travel is quite complicated. This is shown by Table 4, which cross-tabulates what individual respondents were studying at the time of the baseline survey with what they were studying at the time of the final survey,[1] including which year of study within a Degree course they had reached by this end point.

From Table 4 it can be seen that 123 (70%) respondents were enrolled in Degree courses at both the time of the baseline and final surveys. This represents an 84% retention rate of baseline Degree students within Degree courses (excluding five baseline Degree students who were currently enrolled in other courses). However, when year of study was examined it

---

[1] When examining Tables 4 and 5 it should be noted that these only reflect respondents' courses and institutions at two specific points in time (the baseline and the final surveys). Seven respondents had been full-time students outside of these points in time (during the interim survey). This means that the final number of respondents who had not (yet) become a full-time student was only 48 (16% of the sample).

Table 4: Course changes (1999/2000–2001/02)

Current	Baseline Non-student	Other student	NC	HNC	HND	Degree	Total	%
Non-student	50	2	13	11	16	18	110	36
Other student	1	1	0	0	0	0	2	1
NC	1	0	0	0	0	0	1	0
HNC	4	2	3	0	0	1	10	3
HND	9	1	10	1	7	4	32	10
Degree	8	2	4	6	10	123	153	50
First year	3	1	2	2	4	3	15	
Second year	5	1	2	0	2	14	24	
Third year	0	0	0	4	4	106	114	
Total	73	8	30	18	33	146	308	
%	24	3	10	6	11	47		100

was revealed that only 106 of these baseline Degree students had reached their third year of study (a retention rate of 73%). By the time of the final survey, the total number of students who had reached this stage of their career could be inflated by the addition of third year Degree students who had previously been enrolled in other courses at baseline (*n* = 8). Also, other previously non-Degree students were now enrolled in earlier years of study in Degree courses (*n* = 14), as were some respondents who had been previously non-students (*n* = 8).

New students

It can be seen from Table 4 that the overall percentage of students in the sample had decreased over time (from 76% to 64%). This is because, by the end of the project, the numbers discontinuing was exceeding those enrolling for the first time. By the time of the final survey, 23 respondents who had been non-students at the time of the baseline survey (as school-leavers) were now enrolled in full-time education. Six of these new students had been in the labour market for two years (during the interim survey). These new students included 12 respondents who had been in full-time employment at baseline, three who had been in part-time employment only, one who had been on a government training scheme and five who had been unemployed. The level of accessing post-school education among these new students varied across each type of course, but included eight who entered Degree courses (five having

now reached their second year and three having only just enrolled in their first year; see Table 4).

Former students

Moving in the opposite direction were the 60 respondents, who had accessed further or higher education directly on leaving school, but who had become non-students by the time of the final survey (19 discontinuing after one year and 41 after two years). Of those who had left full-time education during the project, 38 were now in full-time employment, 11 were employed part-time only, one was on a government training scheme and 10 were unemployed. The most advanced qualification gained by these ex-students varied, with 15 having gained an HND, 10 an HNC, five an NC and three other FE qualifications (such as SVQ). The remaining 27 had discontinued their education without gaining any new qualifications (although one Degree dropout had since gained vocational qualifications through a government training scheme).

The majority of respondents who gained any qualifications from full-time education during this project had not yet left full-time education. These comprised 16 students in the final survey whose most advanced qualification gained (so far) was an HND, eight an HNC, six an NC and six other FE qualifications. These respondents had either achieved their new qualifications as part of an ongoing course (HNC as part of an

HND) or had now enrolled in a new, usually more advanced, course (such as a Degree).

Educational status

Using Table 4, a simplified categorisation of the various career pathways taken by respondents was created. This was done taking into account any course changes that had occurred between the baseline and final data sweeps (for example, at the time of the interim survey). This produced nine types of student career path, which are hereafter referred to as respondents' educational status at the time of the final data sweep. These educational statuses are defined as follows:

- **Never-students** (n = 48): This group may be considered the least successful, even though some may become students in future (five were expected to be full-time students within the next year and ten were already studying part-time).
- **Straight-to-Degree** students (n =106): This group may be considered the most successful. Although no respondent had yet sat any Degree exams, in this research reaching Degree (third) year is regarded as strongly indicative of likely success (that is, such students are unlikely to leave with nothing).
- **Deferrers** (n = 20): These are the new current students who had previously entered the labour market directly after leaving school, rather than enrolling in full-time education at that time. Respondents who subsequently changed their status again are not included in this category.
- **Progressers** (n = 38, at the time of the final follow up survey): This educational status comprises all current students who had completed a previous course, then enrolled directly into another (usually more advanced) course without entering the labour market. For example, the eight respondents who had reached the third year of a Degree course via HNC or HND studentships.
- **Completers** (n = 28): These are ex-students who had successfully finished their last course, then left full-time education, entering the labour market without advancing into another full-time course.
- **Dropouts** (n = 35): These respondents are ex-students who did not complete their last course, including those who had completed a

previous course, such as obtaining an HNC as part of an unfinished HND.
- **Returners** (n = 14): For some respondents becoming a 'completer' or a 'dropout' was not an inevitable endpoint. These are current students who had returned to full-time education by enrolling in another (usually less advanced) course after a gap (usually of one year) spent in the labour market.
- **Restarts** (n = 14): These are also current students who had enrolled in another course (or at another institution), but, in their case, this was by switching course directly after spending one or two (successful) years in a previous course without entering the labour market, usually by starting back in the first year of an equally advanced course. (Many other respondents made minor subject changes within the same course, without having to restart from an earlier year of study. They are not included in this category.)
- **Repeaters** (n = 5, at the end of the project): These are current students who had been forced to repeat a year of full-time study within the same course.

The latter five groups, 'dropouts', 'completers', 'returners', 'restarts' and 'repeaters' can be regarded as those who have reduced their level of participation in post-school education at some point. When asked to state why this had happened in the questionnaire, respondents provided a variety of reasons, including disliking or choosing the wrong course (n = 28), financial difficulties or debt (n = 11) and the lure of the labour market (n = 8). However, as will be elaborated on in the next chapter, these reasons were often interrelated. (Further details of respondents who reduced their level of participation in full-time education can be seen in Appendix F.)

Although, as we will see, prior achievement was related to which one of these nine categories respondents fell into, it should be noted that this relationship was not automatic, especially among the highest school achievers. For example, of the seven 'straight A' pupils in the sample, only three had gone 'straight-to-Degree', two had become 'restarts', one was a 'deferrer' now only studying towards an Ordinary Degree, and one had become an unemployed 'dropout' despite having successfully studied for two years towards a Degree in Medicine at a distant 'ivy league' institution. In other words, Highers points may

Table 5: Institution changes (1999/2000–2001/02)

Current \ Baseline	Non-student	FE college	New university	Red brick university	Ivy league university	Total	%
Non-student	50	41	12	3	4	110	36
FE college	13	19	4	3	0	39	13
New university	5	12	40	0	2	59	19
First year	3	5	1		0	9	
Second year	2	2	4		1	9	
Third year	0	5	35		1	41	
Red brick university	2	5	1	54	0	62	20
First year	1	1	0	0		2	
Second year	1	4	0	2		7	
Third year	0	0	1	52		53	
Ivy league university	3	3	0	0	32	38	12
First year	0	3			1	4	
Second year	3	0			8	11	
Third year	0	0			23	23	
Total	73	80	57	60	38	308	
%	24	26	19	20	12		100

not always remain the principal governing factor in predicting success within higher education.

Changing institution

The course changes (in terms of qualification being studied for) shown in Table 4 tell only part of the story of the diversity of student career pathways found in this research. As shown in Table 1, different courses are available at different types of institution, so respondents who had changed course may also have changed their institution. For example, completing an FE course then proceeding to higher education, may involve an institutional transition, such as moving from college to university. The pattern of institutional changes between the baseline and the final data sweeps is shown in Table 5.[2]

Although complicated, Table 5 reveals some interesting patterns, not apparent from Table 4. First, the numbers attending each type of university remained remarkably similar throughout.[2] At both the beginning and the end of the project the number of respondents enrolled in an 'ivy league' institution was 38, with numbers attending 'red brick' and 'new' universities also varying little (from 60 to 62 and 57 to 59 respectively). However, it is indicated that it was not always the same individuals who were in attendance throughout the study. 'New' universities in particular seemed to have substantial numbers of respondents leaving (n = 17) or enrolling (n = 19) between these times. Second, although progress from FE college to university is indicated, these transitions were not uniform across the three categories of university. Specifically, those progressing from FE college were able to access 'new' universities directly into Degree (third) year if they had obtained an HND (and into other years with lesser qualifications). Such students could at best only access second year at 'red brick' institutions and were having to start at the very beginning of 'ivy league' university courses. Third, the ratio of Degree-year students to students in their first and second years varied at each type of university. This ratio was greatest at 'red brick' universities (53:9), compared with 'new' (41:18) and in particular 'ivy league' (23:15) institutions. In other words, students attending 'red brick' universities appeared to be faring better in this research than those at 'new' or 'ivy league' universities (this latter finding mirroring the local

---

[2] In Table 5 and in subsequent analyses, the two respondents who attended specialised HE colleges (agricultural college and art school) are coded as 'red brick'; the two who attended more general HE colleges as 'new' university students.

access ratios to institution types detailed in the previous chapter).

Predicting changes in participation

In order to explain why different groups of respondents had enjoyed different levels of success in post-school education a number of statistical analyses (regressions) were conducted. These were designed to see if academic success at the time of the final sample could be predicted from the data gathered two years earlier during the baseline survey of school-leavers. In other words, to see whether underlying socioeconomic disadvantaged governed the likelihood of continued success in higher education.

Level of success

A variable measuring levels of academic success between the baseline and final surveys was constructed. This measure – a seven-point scale – was designed to take account of all the career pathways shown by Tables 4 and 5, including the hierarchy of university types. On this scale, the lowest score (of zero points) was allocated to all non-students who had gained no qualifications since leaving school (n = 57, including 'never-

students' and 'dropouts'). Next (with one point), came the respondents who were either non-students who had gained FE qualifications (that is, 'completers') or were students currently enrolled in FE courses (n = 28). Non-students whose highest qualification obtained on completion was an HNC and students currently studying for an HNC were allocated two points. Also allocated two points were students currently enrolled in the first year of a course (Degree or HND) at a 'new' university. Students enrolled in their second year at 'new' universities were awarded three points, as were first year students at 'red brick' universities. By this process, at the top end of the scale (with six points) were the respondents who had reached the third year of a Degree course at an 'ivy league' institution (n = 23). This points division by university type was done to take into account the differences in likely level of access to a Degree course at each institution for 'progessers' with an HND. A full explanation of how this academic success variable was derived can be seen in Table 6.

The above procedure was duplicated to produce a similar variable measuring level of success at the time of the baseline survey. It was intended to use this latter variable as a control, in order to measure how much each respondent had either increased or decreased their level of participation in higher education over the duration of this

Table 6: Academic success variable

Studentship/course being studied at time of the final survey	Highest qualification gained	Success score	n
Non-student	None	0	57
Highers	Highers	1	28
(G)SVQ	(G)SVQ		
NC	NC		
HNC (HND at baseline)	HNC	2	33
Y1 Degree at FE college			
Y1 Degree at 'new' university			
HND/Y2 Degree at FE college	HND	3	54
Y2 Degree at 'new' university			
Y1 Degree at 'red brick' university			
Y3 Degree at FE college	–	4	49
Y3 Degree at 'new' university			
Y2 Degree at 'red brick' university			
Y1 Degree at 'ivy league' university			
Y3 Degree at 'red brick' university	–	5	64
Y2 Degree at 'ivy league' university			
Y3 Degree at ivy league university	–	6	23

Figure 4: Social class and academic success measure

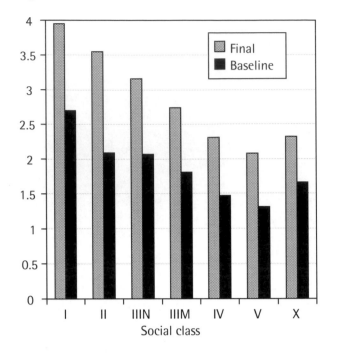

research. As might be expected, this post-school academic success variable displayed a social class gradient that closely mirrored that of school achievement (as measured by Highers points; see Figure 1). This was true at both the time of the baseline and final surveys, indicating that the *more* disadvantaged young people who took part in this research had not 'caught up' with their *relatively* advantaged peers over the duration of the project, as is shown by Figure 4.

To predict academic success across the whole sample, a regression analysis was conducted for *all* 308 respondents with the academic success measure score (at the time of the final survey) as the dependent variable and background demographics (that is, measures of disadvantage) as independent (predictor) variables. This found that, controlling for level of success at baseline, continued success in higher education could be predicted by school achievement (Highers points), having a family history of FE or HE and being female (see Appendix B, Regression 4). In other words, prior academic success (itself a function of disadvantage) and having a family member who had been a full-time student in the past were indicative of continued success across the sample as a whole. Also, male respondents were less likely to have improved on their level academic success over the duration of this research.

This procedure was repeated for all 235 baseline *students only* (see Appendix B, Regression 5). In doing so, it was now possible to predict the academic success variable (at time of the final survey) from both the demographic variables (common to all respondents) and the baseline student-only variables (for example, those concerning student finance, accommodation and courses). Controlling again for initial level of success, a range of variables, mainly relating to prior student characteristics, was found to predict continued academic success:

- school achievement (Highers points);
- thinking that loans other than student loans (for example, bank loans) would *not* be important during their career;[3]
- *longer* daily travel time to institution;
- *less* anticipated final debt;
- thinking that student loans *would be* important during their career;
- having left the parental home; and
- having a family history of FE or HE.

From this, it would appear that, even among those who became students directly after leaving school, prior achievement and having a family member who had previously been a full-time student were still important predictors of likely academic success. However, it was also indicated that debt aversion might play a role. Specifically, those who thought they would get into debt from loans other than student loans (for example, bank loans) during their student career and those who thought they would get into a lot of debt by the end of their studentship were less likely to have been successful. In contrast, those who expected student loans to be important during their student career were more likely to have been successful. Finally, those who had already left their parental home to go to college or university, were found to be have been more successful, as were those who travelled longer distances to their chosen institution every day. These latter findings, concerning student loans, independent living and longer commuting would seem slightly

---

[3] Seven three-point scales measured how important respondents felt a range of sources of income would be to them during their student careers (income from: parents/ family, bursaries, scholarships and other funds, student loans, bank and other loans, paid work and 'extra' income, for example 'fiddling') ranging from 'not important' through 'quite important' to 'very important'.

counterintuitive, as they all would involve greater costs. Potential reasons behind this will be explored in the next chapter.

Finally, this analysis was repeated for the 147 baseline *Degree students only* (see Appendix B, Regression 6). This analysis used the same predictor variables as the previous one, although in this instance it should be noted that all the students involved were more similar (in terms of their course length, system of student finance and likely career pathways and so on). Controlling for initial level of success (in this case type of university only), success among Degree students was predicted by:

- thinking that loans other than student loans (such as bank loans) would *not* be important;
- social class;
- having enrolled in first choice course;
- thinking that 'other' funds (such as scholarships) *would be* important during their student career;
- *not* having been a bursary pupil at school;[4]
- thinking that student loans *would be* important; and
- *longer* daily travel time to institution.

As with all students, Degree students who had thought that loans other than student loans would be important during their career were less successful, while those who thought that student loans would be important were more successful. Again, those who travelled to institutions further away were more likely to be successful. However, only among Degree students, was it found that those with a higher parental social class were more successful. Also in only this instance, those who thought that other student funds (such as scholarships) would be important were also more likely to have been successful; however, Degree students who had received financial assistance at school (as bursary pupils) were less successful. Finally, Degree students who did not enrol in their first choice course (for whatever reason) were also less successful. Interestingly, prior (that is, school) achievement and family history of HE and FE did not feature in this equation. In other words, it would appear that factors relating to student finance, social

class and institution were more important in determining academic success among Degree students in this sample.

As the baseline measure of academic success among Degree students varied only according to type of university initially accessed ('ivy league', 'red brick' or 'new'), it was decided to explore the relationship between continued success and institution further, by conducting a final regression equation with 'straight-to-Degree' status as the dependent variable (see Appendix B, Regression 7). In this analysis, binary variables for each type of university were included as independent (predictor) variables, along with the demographic and student variables used before. This analysis found that students who had gone 'straight-to-Degree' in this sample could be predicted by:

- *not* having enrolled at either a 'new' or an 'ivy league' university;
- thinking that loans 'other' than student loans would *not* be important during their student career; and
- having already taken out a student loan at baseline.

In other words, respondents who had initially enrolled in Degree courses at 'red brick' universities appeared to be faring better than those who had enrolled elsewhere. This was also true of those who had taken out student loans from the outset of their academic career. From this, and from the previous regression, it would appear that, among the better qualified young people in this research, interactions between social class, institution type and debt aversion are the main factors governing the likelihood of continued success in higher education – *not* prior achievement.

Although at first glance the above analyses may seem complicated, several clear trends are already emerging. First, males appeared to be enjoying less success than females. Reduced participation by males comes on top of their pre-existing under-representation in post-compulsory education (detailed in Forsyth and Furlong, 2000). Financial matters, such as (perceptions of) debt, appeared to impact on participation, as did issues relating to choice of course and type of institution. Underlying these was the continued influence of pre-existing achievement. This was represented by Highers points and initial level of

---

4 'Bursary pupil' in this research refers to secondary school pupils who received a bursary for remaining in school beyond the minimum leaving age of 16 years. These are paid to school pupils from low-income families only.

access to higher education as a school-leaver (itself governed primarily by school achievement), which were themselves a function of disadvantage (as shown by Figures 1 and 4). Finally, it is interesting to note that, in the case of Degree students only (for whom level of school achievement was not a significant factor), social class re-emerges as a predictor of academic success. This latter finding implies that students from disadvantaged socioeconomic backgrounds may be faring less well at some types of institution (such as 'ivy league' universities) than at others, regardless of their academic abilities. This is a theme that is explored more qualitatively in the next chapter.

Summary

The pattern of educational pathways in this sample was quite complicated. If obtaining a Degree as soon as possible was taken as the yardstick for full participation in post-school education, then little more than one third of the sample were travelling on this direct route. The remainder could be described as being on one of a number of gradual routes towards this goal (or not). Some respondents had not (yet) entered higher education, but had remained in the labour market; others were moving between the labour market and full-time education; others were making slower progress, either towards or within higher education. What is of interest at this stage is whether all these different pathways are taken through choice or are forced on these young people, either by their levels of ability or as a consequence of their levels of disadvantage.

At this stage, several reasons appeared to be emerging for why some respondents had been successful, while others had not (from both questions asking directly why they had reduced their level of participation and from subsequent statistical analyses). These included financial concerns, being unhappy with courses, being male and coming from a disadvantaged area or family background.

All these themes are explored in greater depth in the next chapter, which details 81 interviews conducted with a cross-section of respondents, some of whom had taken each of the different educational pathways described in this chapter.

Barriers to full participation in further and higher education

Introduction

The previous chapter outlined respondents' pathways towards and within higher education; specifically, whether they had either reduced or increased their level of participation in a variety of ways. To explore the reasons why respondents had taken each of these educational pathways in greater detail, face-to-face interviews were conducted with a sub-sample of disadvantaged young people. A total of 40 interviews were conducted during the spring of 2001 and another 41 young people were interviewed during the spring of 2002. Rather than randomly selecting respondents for these interviews, it was decided to focus on those who had changed their educational status, according to their previous questionnaire data. The selection of interviewees was stratified to include a range of educational statuses (as detailed in Chapter 4). Where possible, particularly disadvantaged young people were selected for interview (especially interviewees in the most successful 'straight-to-Degree' category). By these methods it was intended to ascertain how any background disadvantages (detailed in Chapter 2) or student hardships (detailed in Chapter 3) had precipitated reduced participation among respondents.

Selection of interviewees

All 81 interviewees were full-time students at some point during this research project. In other words, only those young people whose educational status was described as 'never-students' were ineligible for interview. The interviewees comprised 'dropouts' (n = 18), 'completers' (n = 7), 'returners' (n = 5), 'repeaters'

(n = 8), restarts' (n = 5), 'deferrers' (n = 5), 'progressers' (n = 10) and 'straight-to-Degree' (n = 23). It should be noted that this only refers to interviewees' statuses at the time of their interview and that several individuals were able to talk about previous statuses as well. For example, four of the five 'returners' had been 'dropouts', the other had been a 'completer'. This situation is further complicated by the fact that several interviewees had changed their status from the time of the previous the postal questionnaire survey. For example, three individuals selected for interview in the spring of 2001, from October 2000 data, as 'repeaters' (Angus, Cyril and George) had become 'dropouts' by the time they were interviewed, as had one 'restart' (Vivian) and one 'deferrer' (Janet).

Obviously, the 40 2001 interviewees had not yet reached their 'final' educational status. For example, none of the nine termed 'straight-to-Degree' in 2001 were actually in their second year of a Degree course at that point in time. Six of the 2001 interviewees did not respond to the final postal survey and so their final status is unknown. These were two 'repeaters' (Pierce and Sheena), one 'dropout' (Sammy), one 'completer' (Glenn), one 'progresser' (Penny) and one 'straight-to-Degree' (Ben). Of the 34 who did respond again, two 'dropouts' (George and Jean), two 'completers' (Kathleen and Lena) and one 'repeater' (Sinclair) became 'returners' in session 2001-02. Similarly, another 'repeater' (Archie) became a 'dropout' and one 'progresser' (Jinty) became a 'completer' during the year following their interviews. A fuller description of the interviewee selection procedure can be see in Appendix G.

Interviews were conducted in a variety of settings including parental homes, term-time addresses, workplaces and on campuses. All interviews were taped and transcribed before analysis. The interview gave each respondent the opportunity to explain why they were in their current situation and what barriers they had experienced within post-school education. In this chapter, whenever an interviewee's statement is presented their educational status *at the time of interview* is also given. All personal names cited are fictitious, as are those of any schools, home towns or areas of Glasgow. A brief profile of interviewees' educational pathways and demographic backgrounds is given in Appendices H (for 2001) and I (for 2002 interviewees).

Educational disadvantage

School experiences

As indicated in earlier chapters, underlying (lack of) school achievement was the most important factor in determining the initial destinations in post-school education of respondents in this research. Having now left school, predictably interviewees felt that they had underachieved and wished they had 'stuck in' more at the time.

"I wish I had actually stuck in a lot more at school. I realise that, I mean I thought I was doing fine at school, then you realise you don't when you get the two 'D's through and stuff. I wish I'd probably put in more effort." (Callum, 'returner')

"The best thing to do is concentrate on your Highers because they're worth their weight in gold because they can just get you straight in [to university], no messing about with colleges things like that...." (Eleanor, 'returner')

Not all interviewees felt that their underachievement was entirely their own fault. As detailed in Chapter 2, the schools that they had attended were located in areas of disadvantage; such schools could be under-resourced, especially in terms of provision for (the few) aspiring or high achieving pupils. On meeting their university classmates, interviewees became aware of this underlying disadvantage.

"You get schools that offer ... like you can do Highers in Latin and Highers in Classics and you don't get that opportunity at schools like ours and we do not have any facilities like this. I was speaking to a girl who is from England and she said [her's] is quite a good school, but they're getting money thrown at them and our school can barely afford the teachers, it's not very fair at all." (Elspeth, 'deferrer')

"I did want to try Sixth Year Studies English but there wasn't enough staff, so I was not happy about that. You know it would have gave me a head start. There is nothing you can do, I mean, schools, staff, stuff ... so you sort of feel ... well, why do I bother?" (Archie, 'repeater')

The schools in which respondents were recruited all had below the Scottish national average level of leavers entering higher education. As such, it may be the case that some of these schools have less time to devote to advising aspiring pupils than would be the case in other schools (with more 'middle class' catchment areas). This may, in part, explain one of the most recurring themes among interviewees, which was that they felt that they had been poorly advised at school when making their choices for post-school education. Some interviewees felt that this had created a 'knock on' effect, which had ultimately reduced their level of participation.

"I think that I didn't get really enough information on any careers or anything like that in school. If I did, like, even if they had something that could tell us information on different careers, I would be able to have made an informed decision. I think I would probably be at uni right now if I had got more information in school." (Kathleen, 'completer')

"I was swithering over whether to do the Degree or the Diploma and nobody could tell me the difference and in the end I wish I had done the Diploma." (Kirsten, 'dropout')

Some interviewees felt that they had suffered from their schools' guidance staff concentrating on grooming only a select few pupils for higher education.

"I think it concentrated more on the brighter pupils and they just thought if you werenae bright enough you didnae get as much help." (Frances, 'progresser')

However, some of these 'brighter pupils' also felt that the 'lower aspirations' prevalent at the kind of school that they had attended did not cater for their needs.

"I remember being like in sort of fifth or sixth year [at school] when we were picking our Highers – how many we were doing and things – and they were like, 'Five's an awful lot to be doing. Are you sure you want to do five?' But you have to do five to get in to do Medicine – you have to pass them in fifth year. Everybody sort of treated it as maybe like your expectations of yourself are too high and I think that's the wrong way that the school should be doing things.... I think that the expectations that everybody at the school has of you are quite low. Like, at our school, I felt there was a big emphasis on how to type ... Sciences weren't the priority that I thought that they should have been, so I had to crash my Higher Biology." (Ellen, 'straight-to-Degree')

The UCAS options class, in which respondents chose which higher education courses to apply for, was identified as a particular problem by many interviewees, who felt they had been left to decide their future careers without adequate supervision.

"It was just ten minutes out of class at secondary and I went down and I wrote stupid things like Gynaecology and Zoology, I really did make an arse of it." (Callum, 'returner')

"We were always told at school it's November or whatever – we have to have the UCAS forms in very early. And I thought well that's it, it's too late to apply through UCAS, but in fact it wasn't, because 'Emily' applied through clearing – April or something – and 'Prentice' was on the phone to UCAS this week and they said the cut-off date is actually June – 'we just advise it for November'. And I didn't even realise that when I got a knock-back from art

school, so I might have went to uni instead of college." (Dorothy, 'progresser')

Again, it was some of the most talented individuals who felt that they had suffered from a lack of advice in choosing courses at this stage.

"I went to the careers officer I spoke to you about, and the guidance teacher in the school, aye, in 'Eileanbeg' [remote area], before I left school, and every time I asked anyone for advice they just looked at my grades and went, 'Oh you've got five 'A's, you don't need any advice, you can do anything you want'. And that was the problem, that I didn't really know what I wanted to do and I needed someone to advise me.... I think if I had known that [Medicine] was going to be so specialised and difficult to get out of then I probably wouldn't have done it, I'd really maybe have done a science Degree instead." (Jessie, 'dropout')

This lack of information was a particular problem for the kind of young people in this sample, many of whom were the first in their family to have entered post-school education and who relied on their schools to provide such advice.

"I wish there was some way of getting experience about your course.... I just think it's too hard to choose. Some people know – some people know their path in life and they want to do this, you know, maybe they have friends and family that do it and that's why they want to do it." (Evelyn, 'dropout')

This situation is clearly a disadvantage, as even a very limited family history of further or higher education could be very beneficial for those who had some.

"He [father] was a mature student. He put me off on the right track to uni. The rest of my family who have not been, you know, working class, was working.... He just worked his way – working for Kaeverna [shipyard].... Engineering put him through a four-year course." (Archie, 'repeater')

For those with no family history, even a family friend could fulfil this influential role.

"My mum's friend, she's an English teacher, she is quite helpful, she's been through uni. It was her that really pushed me to go." (Cecilia, 'straight-to-Degree')

Although few interviewees had parents who had been to college or university, several had older siblings who were recent students. These 'trail-blazers' could be a great help, as interviewees could learn from the mistakes made by the first to go.

"My big brother goes, but my mum and dad never went.... This is his third time at uni, so, but he's doing a lot better this time ... this year he seems to be doing better than me. But I mean he encourages me and my mum and dad encourage me ... he was here ['red brick' university] originally, but just spent his time at the shops most of time, so I keep away from that." (Laurie, 'straight-to-Degree')

"See if I was an only child, I was clueless, do you know what I mean? I had to ask my brothers, 'cos they had already been through it all, and the likes of my friends and that. I was thinking, it's just by chance sometimes that you find out things and that's ridiculous." (Kathleen, 'completer')

Post-school experiences

As well as not providing enough information on choices within post-school education, many interviewees also felt that their school could have done more to prepare them for the different teaching methods used at university or college.

"They do too much for you at school ... everything's done for you. I don't know what it is, but know how when you go to uni everything just like ... you have got to do so much yourself, you're so alone. But when you were at school you don't realise how much.... If they made you a bit more independent in fifth and sixth year I think you could cope with uni more." (Vivian, 'dropout')

"School kind of mollycoddled you more.... Like, they would, like, help you all the time – make sure, like – because we were the brainier pupils they would, like, take more

to do with us. But when you're here ['red brick' university] everybody is just treated the same...." (Laurie, 'straight-to-Degree')

Others expressed surprise at the lack of difficulty or workload involved with Degree education. This appears to be a function of the lack of quality advice, information or encouragement received from school or other sources. It seems likely that such misinformation could act as a barrier to some potential students.

"Everything's better than I expected it to be here ['red brick' university]. I thought – I didn't expect this to be like this at all, I thought it would be a lot harder, I didn't think I would be able to do it or that.... No, it's just – I'm quite intimidated by the whole university thing; 'intellectual' [posh voice] thing, you know? I don't think I'm sort of that grade but...." (Eleanor, 'returner')

This belief, that university is too hard or too much work, is also linked back to schools only pushing the more able pupils towards higher education and is likely to adversely effect the aspirations and confidence of all but the most able young people.

"People going to uni would be represented ... shown to a lot of people at my school (I know this from being there) as something that only the people that are quite clever get to do, and that's just nonsense – it's just wrong. I think they have such big ideals of what uni is and they're just not. I mean, see the amount of work you can do here ['ivy league' university] and get away with, it is amazing." (Rachel, 'restart')

Perhaps the greatest surprise for interviewees who enrolled in higher education was the amount of apparently free time that was involved with independent study methods. There is clearly a need for schools to take extra time in preparing potential students for this eventuality. This was a common complaint from interviewees.

"You got plenty information on things like fees and loans and stuff but not actually about student life – about what goes on when you go there. Like having a lecture like say 10 to 11pm and then having like 2 hours to wait until another lecture that kind of thing." (Joe, 'dropout')

"With the timetable I think there was a lot of free time. Four hours between lectures and such like, it was very sparse.... Yeah, because coming out of school, it's like free periods, so you tend to abuse it." (George, 'dropout')

The widespread lack of preparedness for student timetable management had a knock-on effect into other areas of the lives of these disadvantaged students. Many interviewees acknowledged that they had failed to use this time productively – treating as it recreational rather than study time. Such poor time management often resulted in both an increase in spending and a decrease in time spent studying, for example, through unplanned trips to the shops, pub or student union bar. Although drinking is often regarded as a common student pastime, clearly there are extra pitfalls for disadvantaged students, who are likely to be on more limited budgets than their classmates (and perhaps less au fait with alcohol). In any event, the consumption of alcohol between lectures is hardly conducive to study.

"Some of the classes you had, like, four hours in between, so it was a waste of time. I ended up going to the pub and no' going to your next lecture." (Jean, 'dropout')

Missing lectures because of drinking sessions was also connected to the behaviour of peers. In some cases this involved following school peers, many of whom were also finding it difficult to manage their student lifestyle. Resisting this old schoolfriend peer pressure 'domino effect' was clearly important to successful studying.

"Right, there was a friend of mine, who I got involved with, that kind of sidetracked me at the same time as the union did as well. He was a schoolfriend. He actually started college, which he then quit, and then it ... basically the lack of communication between the two of us, that basically I wanted to be more a part of that, actually, so I did." (George, 'dropout')

"Well my friend's at Glasgow Uni ['ivy league'] and she's no' doing very well at all. So kinda, like, she'll just no' bother going

and she'll kinda say, 'Do you [want to?] come here with me?', instead of going and stuff like that and kinda pull me back. But I try no' to do it and say 'no'." (Laurie, 'straight-to-Degree')

Whereas socialising with peers met at college or university may seem a more positive step, this could also present similar pitfalls. For example, one respondent ended up spending too much time attempting to 'fit in' with his new (more affluent) classmates.

"You just get dragged in, it is just, like, we will go for one [drink] and then it becomes into a night out and then that's you no' studying that night and feel a bit rough the next day and it continues up to the weekend.... Just having to ... having to just go along. If you don't go then you're sort of ... won't say outcast – that's too strong again – but you have to kind of go along to be sociable.... In my course, well, too much free time in that aspect sometimes – you don't know what to do with it. In terms of student life and all that, there is never enough." (Archie, 'repeater')

Student social life and networks

Although some interviewees felt that too much socialising had hampered their student career, as time passed, more interviewees felt that they were missing out on a student social life and other youthful activities in order to survive higher education. This could be for a variety of reasons, including financial difficulties, fatigue and time constraints. For some, this 'missing out' was no more than an annoyance, as they were aware that their lives did not resemble the popular stereotype of students.

"I don't think that I get involved so much in the social life because I generally am tired a lot. I do go to the student union occasionally, but it's not a big part of it.... Sometimes [I felt I missed out] because I mean if I'm going to be labelled a 'layabout student' I'd like to live up to it. [...] It would be nice, but I really don't have the energy a lot of the time." (Christel, 'straight-to-Degree')

"I couldn't afford to, I mean, they say that students go out boozing and everything, but then you just can't afford to, quite frankly." (Winnie, 'completer')

On the other hand, some were determined not to misspend their youth, by ensuring that they participated fully in student social activities, no matter what the cost.

"I'm also at Footlights – one of the societies – and I think that helps me be more at ease, and, like, you'll get people I know who, like, go to rehearsals on their scooters and it is quite funny. I suppose you'd sort of feel a bit bitter if you'd, like, no money, because it's a totally different experience if you've got money at university. That's why I tend not to worry about money. I don't think I'd miss out – I know I'm in loads of debt but I'll worry about it later." (Malcolm, 'straight-to-Degree').

For such individuals, social life was seen not only as being as important as the academic aspects of student life but also as something which aided it, either by helping the interviewee to 'fit in' or by acting as a release from the pressures of study. However, other interviewees felt that they were being excluded from this important part of their lives. This could erode morale and even commitment to study.

"I didn't really get involved in the social life to be quite honest, because I was actually working most of the time. And I was from 'Glenburgh' [large town], so every time I was finishing college I was going home to go to work, so I kind of ... socialising and stuff I tended to stick with my friends that I had from school.... I do [feel I missed out] because a lot of the time all the guys who were getting the train in, it was, 'Oh yeah, we're going to the pub', and I was driving home in the car thinking, 'God I hate this'." (Loretta, 'dropout')

"That was one of the reasons I left – I never really enjoyed it that much.... The subject that I was studying, I really enjoyed, and I learned a lot out of that.... Glasgow ['ivy league'] is a dead old uni and it's a dead old ... erm, you know what I'm trying to say, eh? It was a wee bit too snobbish for me in some ways ... everybody was, you know, walking aboot with their heid up there, and the couple of pals that I'd got close to, they were never in at the same time as us. A lot of the time I found myself just wandering about myself, going tae the library, and didnae like that. Everybody talks about their student life, you know, you're supposed to be going out getting pissed every night and I never found any of that." (Evelyn, 'dropout')

Like Evelyn, many interviewees were now encountering more affluent people of their own age for the first time, which could be a novel or an unpleasant experience. This was compounded by the fact that few from schools like theirs access university.

"It can be quite cliquey at times ... partly because, obviously, I was the only person that came from my school to do my course and there was a few people in the same position, but mostly people on my course already knew at least one other person on the course." (Colleen, 'straight-to Degree')

"More than half of them were English and the majority of them were from quite rich families, and a lot of them were from the families of doctors. And so I felt a wee bit out of place because like I don't really know anybody that's a doctor even, and I come from a sort of, not a really poor family but, compared with them, yeah." (Jessie, 'dropout')

Some interviewees, who had trouble fitting in with this new peer group sought out any students from similar (socioeconomic) backgrounds to themselves.

"I have made a lot more friends within Medicine [this year]. So that's ... I think that helps the course as well because you want to come in. Because before you were dreading coming in, that kind of thing. So probably, oddly enough, as the social life has improved, your work has improved.... I mix with a different group. I've met a couple of people – one's from 'Fernburgh' [large town], she repeated first year so she didn't really know many people – then there's a couple of girls – they've got married and stuff.... They are more down to earth and things." (Ellen, 'straight-to-Degree')

"There's definitely a lot more middle class people and I find that quite strange compared to 'Lochbeg' [remote area]. And there's a lot of, I don't know, we call them 'yahs'. There's a lot of them – they are quite yucky.... It sounds bad – their accents – and they're loud and they just think they're wonderful and they just deny it. But not everyone ... there's not many people that are actually like that and my friends are nicer." (Elspeth, 'deferrer')

In complete contrast to this, other interviewees had no trouble 'fitting in'. They viewed meeting these new more affluent peers as a positive experience, which both broadened their horizons and allowed them to interact with people more (academically) like themselves than would be possible in their home areas.

"I'm living with two people in my flat who went to, like, public school, single-sex schools, but it's a really mixed.... You meet so many different people, it kind of opens your eyes to the way other people live." (Cecilia, 'straight-to-Degree')

"Most of them go to private schools; there is quite a high degree of English ones as well. Yeah, I would say there is quite a lot in Edinburgh ['ivy league']. Well, Edinburgh is quite a pretentious university anyway – my course more so.... I have more in common with people at university than I did with people at school." (Malcolm, 'straight-to-Degree')

Interviewees who were neither able to fit in, nor find others from their own background, were in danger of becoming socially isolated, which again could lower morale and commitment to continuing with higher education.

"Aye they were nice, but different just.... I don't think I was very studenty and they were more studenty, like. I don't know, I just don't think I fitted in. I don't know, they were just like a typical student – they would buy, like, different clothes, like, just cheap clothes." (Jean, 'dropout')

"Some of them [I liked], but some of them were nutters, man.... Just pure spaced-out, especially ... just the way they dressed them all.... I don't know, they're just hippyish and all that. Aye, I got on wi' ... just guys that were into fitba' an' all that, and are okay for a laugh." (Kieran, 'dropout')

Meeting these new peers could also negatively effect interviewees' levels of commitment and confidence by making them more aware of their relative economic disadvantage. For example, the perception that their more affluent classmates had a greater chance of academic success at the end of the day, simply because of their families' greater levels of income and prior experience of higher education.

"It's just, like, they've just got more money behind them and their parents have been to uni whatever, so they know what they're doing." (Laurie, 'straight-to-Degree').

"A lot of them didn't have jobs and they were all very well off. Like, they could study at night, if you know what I mean." (Vivian, 'dropout')

Economic disadvantage

Budgeting against hardship

The negative financial experiences of interviewees extended well beyond any constraints to their social lives. Many interviewees had no previous experience of handling their personal finances and had found it difficult to cope with the economics of student life on their limited incomes. This involved budgeting income such as loans, wages and family resources against expenditure on items such as accommodation, travel and paying off debt. In some cases, this could leave little to survive on, let alone socialise. In the most extreme cases, sheer lack of funds alone could result in some students leaving education. This was particularly the case with interviewees enrolled in further education courses funded only by bursaries (such as NC), who were unable to access student loans to complete their courses if their bursaries were insufficient to cover their living costs.

"Well I only had two weeks to go, as I says, and I never had any bursary or anything like that. Bursaries ran out, so I could not afford to go, so I ended up leaving it." (Lara, 'dropout')

"I'm no' going to go back ken? It's just ... it's the money, I cannae afford to go.... I'd done illustration last year and it was the same thing – I got to the end of the year and I just started running out of money and I didnae finish the course." (Angus, 'dropout')

Interviewees who were in receipt of student loans also stated that they were suffering financial hardship. Even those on maximum loans could feel that these were insufficient to meet their living costs, let alone study costs.

"The loan is just not enough – even the maximum amount is not enough and you are talking, like, a grand each. What I'm taking just now is, basically, it translates to about a grand each time and that's just, like, that leaves me with, actually that leaves me in debt, with no money for food, so it's very hard to keep the money going." (Pierce, 'repeater')

For most interviewees, expenditure directly related to their studies was restricted to books. However, those on more specialised or prestigious courses had extra costs relating to materials, equipment, placements or field trips. These costs alone could deter less affluent students from continuing on such courses.

"It [architecture] is very expensive as well. I was thinking of continuing it and it cost a lot of money at the end of the day. Unlike the other courses where you are doing Maths, English, Geography or whatever. You might not have to put out as much money on books and stuff, but that you have to spend a lot on art materials – other stuff: equipment – and I just thought, I'm going to get out. I feel it's very unlikely that I am going to do another year of this or continue this course, and I just thought I don't want to spend more money on something that I don't want to continue.... If that had not been an issue I would probably would have stayed on and done the year to see how I got on, but I felt guilty, I thought, and I said to my dad, I said, 'I don't want to spend your money – waste your money'." (Muneer, 'restart')

As might be expected, most respondents in this research were unable to rely on their parents to finance their student lives. However, many interviewees had entered into informal arrangements in which their families played an important role in their budget, alongside student finance and other income sources.

"Well I've had two loans in the first two years I'm here ['new' university]. It's the top loan – £3,200 each year – but I've also got a part-time job, but I can only ... it's only Tuesday, Wednesday and Thursday, and it is only three hours a night, so it is nine hours a week, but really it is not a lot.... But I'm getting by because I am not paying dig money because my mum and dad are letting me off with it just now." (Ben, 'straight-to-Degree')

During interviews, it became clear that the magnitude of economic hardship faced by students could be gauged by the nature of their financial relationship with their family. Some, like Ben, above (who was means tested at a maximum loan allowance), were in a 'give nothing/receive nothing' situation, in cash terms. Many others were not so fortunate and felt obliged to give a proportion of their income from student loans and bursaries *to* their parents.

"Well, I mean, I've paid dig money since I was at school, fae my bursaries, so I gave part of my loan to my mum and dad." (Loretta, 'dropout')

"Well it's no' so much. My mum, it's just like she's a single parent and I've got a ten-year-old sister, so it's, yeah, I feel better contributing.... Oh, but there are times when she won't take money, the amount differs. It's, she doesn't like taking money, but because of the way it is...." (Christel, 'straight-to-Degree')

Being both a student and 'breadwinner' could have a knock-on effect to other career choices. For example, if parents or other family become economically dependent on the student, this could tie him or her to a job, preventing them from moving into student accommodation, further limiting their choices (for example, of which institution to attend).

"See I help my mum out along with the rent and stuff like that, so, as I say, I've got a full-time job to keep that going. I've got a car to run as well. So I cannae really afford to move out the house at the moment."
(Jimmy, 'restart')

Accommodation and travel

The main way in which families could offer support was by minimising food and accommodation costs. This, in part, explains why so few respondents had opted to leave their parental home while studying. As might be expected, those who did move out into student accommodation found that this was their main source of expenditure.

"I'm absolutely skint. I'm on the loans – I've got a full loan and it is not enough to live on because the rent on the student flats is quite high and it doesnae leave you much." (Cecilia, 'straight-to-Degree')

Interviewees from the remote area, who did not have the option of living at home, felt particularly penalised by the cost of independent living.

"I know people who do live with their parents, on my course, and they actually have the loan as well. So they are set up. They can save it if they want to go out, but it is very difficult having to pay for accommodation and everything else."
(Pierce, 'repeater')

However, respondents who remained in their parental homes often found that commuting could also prove expensive, particularly for those from the small town study area, who also felt disadvantaged by geography.

"Well, see, the bursary I get is £39 a month and my bus fares are £6.50 a day so it just doesn't add up. I cannae work it out.... There's folk stay in Glasgow and they get like £108 and they can walk tae the college, I don't ken how that makes sense, I cannae work that out." (Angus, 'dropout')

Commuting students, again particularly those from the small towns, also found their study time could be restricted by the lack of public transport provision. Obviously, students in such situations could benefit from living closer to their place of study.

"I've got to come home, like, five o'clock, and I just get the train so I can stay up later. But its, like, the last bus is quarter to six to come back out to 'Coaltoun', so if I miss it, then that's me had it. So I can only stay until about five to study." (Jock, 'repeater')

The non-academic environment of the parental home itself could place further restrictions on studying for many, such as these two interviewees (both of whom had complained about the limited availability of public transport to their institutions).

"I cannae do them [assessments] at home. I've got a wee brother that runs about and I just cannae get peace in the house to do them." (Angus, 'dropout')

"I was in my old bedroom which was a tiny wee box room – there was no room for a desk in it. So if I was to work in the house I'd have to do work downstairs in the living room, but obviously the telly was on and there was five of us in quite a small house." (Ellen, 'straight-to-Degree')

Some interviewees had solved this accommodation versus travel dilemma by investing their debts into buying a car, such as this interviewee, who had previously faced a multi-staged journey to university via public transport.

"I do have the car – I'd rather fork out and have a car and stay here [parental home].... I think I'd get into more debt – it [accommodation] just costs too much really.... Because my friends who have gone way, they're in more debt than me, they're not enjoying it, and at least I've got the car to show for it at the moment. I mean they havenae got anything, are always skint as well. I'm no' gonnae move out." (Nell, 'straight-to-Degree')

Nevertheless, the main costs of commuting, rather than living in student accommodation, are the constraints on study time this can cause. This situation was often compounded by students choosing cheaper modes of transport, which not only tended to take longer but also tended to be less conducive to studying, such as taking the bus rather than the train, walking rather than taking the bus and choosing to travel outside peak hours when fares were cheaper.

"Well, I need to get up at 6 o'clock – half 6 at the latest – to get up to be in here for 9 o'clock. That's, like, an hour and 45 minutes on the way in, maybe an hour or more on the way and back.... Well, it's really, really dear – it's £5.40 if I'm in here before 9 o'clock." (Lexy, 'repeater' [only pays half of £40 per week council house rent, shared with boyfriend in home town])

As well as using up a lot of potential study time, long-distance commuting also could make interviewees fatigued, especially if it clashed with paid employment.

"I was getting up at, like, half 5 in the morning. I'd to get my bus, to get my train, then I'd to get my tube and the tube in the morning was an absolute nightmare." I was in 9 'til 5, Monday to Friday. I've got a full-time job that I'm doing while I'm at uni as well, so it's heavy going." (Jimmy, 'restart')

Paid employment

Inevitably, many students reluctantly saw taking on a part-time (or even a full-time) job (or jobs) as the only way to alleviate their financial woes.

"I'm going to have to go out and get a job.... I mean, I'm not getting another loan payment 'til May and it'll be pretty tight until then.... I don't know about a lot of folk, but I find it hard to get motivated to study, let alone study and work." (Catriona, 'straight-to-Degree')

Once again, the careers of students who also acted as a breadwinners for their families were particularly vulnerable to this becoming a barrier to full-time education.

"Right now I'm having to work two jobs [administration and pizza delivery] because I've got ... my girlfriend's just had a wee baby. She's also ... she's got another wee boy as well and I'm kind of like his dad. So the way I see is, like, trying to support the two of them as well, so it's kind of ... I've had to take on this other job as well as doing uni. Having to do 10 hours during the week, from between 9 'til 5, and then having to work at night as well." (Shug, 'progresser')

As well as eroding study time, there was also the danger that taking on too much paid work could increase fatigue and hinder academic performance.

"I was doing nightshift on a Saturday night recovering on the Sunday and I was not recovered enough for college in the Monday.... Well, we were sitting in lectures maybe two-, three-hours long, you know, and I was trying to concentrate, but it was ... I was that knackered." (Trevor, 'dropout')

"I'm working between 40 and 45 hours a week at the moment and my college course is ... works out about 18 hours. So I'm going home and I'm sleeping, if not I'm studying, you know, it's quite heavy going.... I'm never ... I've never been so tired. Even if I'm tired I'll come in and I've never fallen asleep in class." (Libby, 'deferrer')

As well as fatigue, many interviewees found that part-time jobs could actually clash with class time. This left students with another dilemma.

"Well it was constantly, I mean, it was going to college – I was actually trying to skip classes to go oot to get to work to get that, just that extra bit. I mean, the money was crap as it was, but still you had to get as much as you could." (Loretta, 'dropout')

If work was either seen as imperative or was chosen over class attendance, this could have direct negative consequences for a student's career.

"It kind of was a waste of a year. I was doing training for the job in the supermarket and I missed a week [at college] and when I come back they were doing a six-month project, four of us, two of them actually changed the content so that I was not really part of it. I kind of blame it [failing] on that a wee bit." (Glenn, 'completer')

"The job has tae win 'cos I need the money." (Logan, 'repeater')

Others in this situation reluctantly gave up their jobs, rather than lose out on class time, despite being aware of the hardships that this could incur.

It's hard, it's really hard. It's, like, you find a part-time job and then uni kicks in, and it's like you've loads of work to do, so you end up missing hours, end up just saying to the job, 'nah, I can't stay anymore, I've got too much uni stuff to do'.... Oh, you huvtae, but sometimes you just huvtae. I mean, when you get a job and you're trying to keep a job, that you put the hours in as well, but it's just a loada hassle. I mean, it costs money travelling between here [campus], the job and your house – costs even more money.... Yeah, definitely, you need to give up work tae go to uni. I wouldn't give up uni to go to work – there's just no point, 'cos this is my career." (Fergus, 'straight-to-Degree')

"Last year I was working. In the first two years of the uni I was working quite a lot of hours – ended up in hospital for a week due tae stress. So I had tae give up that job and now I'm working like half the hours that I was working before and I'm just *constantly* trying to get money fae places.... I get a loan – ahah! – and I get a [Robertson Trust] scholarship as well, and at the moment I'm trying to get my [absent] dad to pay me money – hah!" (Annie, 'restart')

As might be expected, those enrolled in the most advanced or prestigious (and costly) courses were those with least time available to devote to part-time work. This was a factor for one student interviewed who switched to a less prestigious course.

I have got a job [in new course]. In Architecture [previous course] you can't have a job – you have to [do course] work constantly." (Muneer, 'restart')

As time in higher education passed and their courses became more advanced, this problem began to hit more students. In other words, financial needs (which could be alleviated by paid work) increased in line with study time requirements.

"It's been difficult this year. I'm in more debt this year than I was in first and second Year.... I think first and second year it was ... the course was easier – well first year definitely was easy. And I never really worked hard at the course and I could ... the job I was in [Rocksteady] I could work as much as I wanted to really, so I didn't find money a problem. Second year I probably used up my ... all of the money I'd built up kind of thing, and then now that I'm in third year I'm just in debt.... I can't afford to work as much, as in, like, for money, because I have to study a lot more – the course is just a lot more intense." (Rab, 'straight-to-Degree')

Once again, it was those who had enrolled in the most prestigious courses, such as in Medicine in which there is a summer term, who were most adversely effected.

"Money is by far the biggest problem. In the first year I worked and that was quite hard going.... When I got into second year the course goes up quite a few notches so I had to give it up. So I was just living at home, and my parents don't give me any money at all, so that's the hardest thing. And then because I'd saved up some money second year wasn't so bad. But this year I was already maxed-out on my overdraft at the beginning of the year, so I don't know what I'm going to do in the summer. I can't get a summer job because I've got a term this summer, but you can get bank loans out now apparently." (Ellen, 'straight-to-Degree')

Ultimately, exam time presented the biggest potential clash between paid work and study needs, particularly as many exams were set around Christmas time, when students found themselves under extraordinary financial stress.

"At Christmas time, when I was working, they [Asda] were asking me tae dae overtime, and you need the money obviously because it's Christmas time, but then you've got exams to study for in January. So I'm sort of blaming that on why I failed two of my exams in January there. So I'm trying to get my hours cut back and all." (Lizzie, 'progresser')

Lizzie's account also highlights another problem – that of employers who may exact pressure on vulnerable 'hard up' students to work extra hours.

"I was working down home [near her Glasgow flat], because I was travelling, it was taking up a lot of time anyway, and I was working for Gala Bingo. It was in 'Kilntoun' [small town], so I was travelling again in and out of my work, and they were asking me to take time off college to come in and work, and if I did it one week they'd expect you to do it the next week...." (Dorothy, 'progresser')

A number of strategies were adopted to get around employers' demands at exam time without losing a job, such as claiming exams as holidays or 'sickies'.

"I usually have holidays, so I usually maybe get the week off just before exams and stuff." (Audrey, 'straight-to-Degree')

"[At exam time] I can, I usually either phone in sick or arrange time off." (Christel, 'straight-to-Degree')

Through increased hours, involvement with employers or fellow employees and by being financially dependent on paid employment, there was clearly a potential for the identity of the respondent to become comprised between that of 'working student' and that of 'student worker'. This in itself could distract from student life, which some recognised in time, but which led to others losing commitment to continued study.

"I felt it was creating too much of a distraction from my studies. It was giving me this whole other ... like, I was starting to work [in shop] straight after uni when I should have been studying; I was socialising with people from work and I shouldn't have been doing because they are in a sort of different atmosphere to students are and they maybe wouldn't appreciate

that I would be studying when they were wanting to do things like that." (Rachel, 'restart')

"For my January exams in second year I was on course, you know, to pick any Degree that I could through modules. Then we stopped for Easter. I got that job [nightclub], I was working during the day [bookmakers] and I wasnae doing any [course] work. And I'm the sort of person – I need to keep doing work, you know, I need to keep doing something everyday, reading something everyday, just so that – no' learn anything – just so that I'm used to sitting down and studying. So when I got back after the month, I was tired as well fae working in 'Rhea' [nightclub], I found myself ... I wasnae getting up and going into uni in the morning. So a wee bit of both, the job and I lost my motivation just because I wasnae putting the work in...." (Evelyn, 'dropout')

Keeping working hours to the weekend was one way of successfully separating work and study. This was one reason why so many respondents had kept the same part-time job since their schooldays. The problem with this is that students who had left the parental home now had to travel from their term-time address to work.

"I am quite fortunate because I've got myself quite a good part-time job. I've got two part-time job's actually – I work on a Saturday and I make £40 doing that and I work on a Friday night making £60 doing that, hosting kareoke shows ... that's in 'Eileanbeg' [remote area]. I go home every week for that, so, but that's me making £100 a week doing that." (Eleanor, 'returner')

Eleanor was indeed fortunate, because, as might be expected, students from deprived areas found it difficult to find *any* part-time employment during term time.

"There is nothing about here [small town]. See, I need to travel to go to it and I have no car and a lot of folk willnae take you unless you have got transport." (Angus, 'dropout')

Similarly, some interviewees were unable to find any paid employment outside term time from which savings could be have been made. This was particularly the case with those from the small town study area where opportunities for seasonal employment, such as tourism, were non-existent.

"I've had quite a large overdraft this year because I wasn't working during the summer.... Just because of the lack of jobs really, while I was staying down in 'Minetoun' [small town] and, I mean, it's wee communities – wee villages – there's not a lot of jobs." (Dorothy, 'progresser')

"I tried [to get a job] when I was at home over the summer, but being in 'Coaltoun' [small town] there isnae really much option of one." (Cecilia, 'straight-to-Degree')

For disadvantaged students who lacked income from paid employment the other option for financing their career was taking on debt, such as student loans.

Debt

The main financial concern of many interviewees was the prospect of getting into debt. This was a particularly daunting prospect for many students in this research, whose family and friends also had little experience of this situation.

"The money aspect – more borrowing, more debt – that is the biggest, I think, that's probably the biggest part of it for any student. The only thing that my friends are coming away with is, 'Look at all the debt you are getting into and what is it for?', you know, 'You're going to pay this back for years and years and years'." (Gregor, 'deferrer')

Fear of debt could even act as deterrent to participating in higher education in the first place, such as for this successful NC (bursary-funded) student who forewent the opportunity to progress to a more advanced (loan-funded) course.

"They offered me go on for higher [HNC], but I stopped because I didn't want the loans.... I would rather not have money

against my name saying that I owed." (Winnie, 'completer')

For those who had enrolled in higher education, it was the cumulative amount of debt that they were accruing, which was their chief concern.

"I've got a full student loan, so it's okay, but I have to pay all that back. I don't get any support from mum and dad and I don't think it's fair that because of that I have to get ... I will be £15,000 in debt by the time I'm done.... I'll worry about the debt because, like I said, when I come out it's going to be £15,000 and then you've got to think about buying a house and getting decent jobs." (Elspeth, 'deferrer')

"It's nearly enough the price of a house I'm going to be in debt by the time that I'm finished." (Logan, 'repeater' [the house price being a fact in her small town])

This left many interviewees in the demoralising situation in which they saw themselves as working while being a student to minimise debt and then working after they graduated to pay off this debt, rather than enjoying the 'fruits of their labours'.

"That's [debt] probably my only main concern. I think that's probably it. In the call-centre that I work in there's a lot of people that I know that were at uni and have dropped out and started working in the call-centre. And I think that the major influence on that was probably the amount of debt that they were getting theirsel's into with the loans. I mean, I know people that are nine grand, twelve grand in debt with student loans, and I couldnae sleep at night if I was like that.... When I graduate I want to have money and I want to appreciate the fruits of my labour. I don't want to have to put half of it back into paying off my loans." (Jimmy, 'restart')

For those who were not confident about running up such substantial long-term debts, this could ultimately become a factor which led to reduced participation.

"I did like it [university], but just no' having any money, I didn't like that.... I just kept thinking, like, I was going to be in what,

£12,000 worth of debt if I stayed on." (Jean, 'dropout')

Once a disadvantaged student had got over the first psychological barrier, and actually started taking out loans, this 'fear of debt' was usually not sufficient in itself to lead to reduced participation in higher education. However, when steadily accumulating debt was coupled with other factors, such as bad course choice or employment prospects, this was enough to 'panic' the interviewee into dropping out or early completion.

> "Probably the biggest factor why I left the college, well, my mum and dad don't work so there isn't a lot of kind of financial support at home. Plus the student loans, the fact of getting into debt every year and then you aren't guaranteed a job at the end of it. That's what panicked me the most, because I know people that are now doing the same job as I am [call-centre], they've got a Degree under their belt and all this debt on top of them." (Loretta, 'dropout')

Fear of debt accumulation, was yet another problem that was most acute among those enrolled in more advanced or prestigious (and longer) courses, as they were likely to have to take out the greatest number of student loans.

> "Well, at the time, because everybody was taking out loans, it didn't bother me, because I thought that everyone is going to be in the same position, but, I don't know. It definitely had an effect on whether I stayed on or not, because I was thinking that if I was staying on to study something that I wasn't that interested in [Medicine] and getting into debt at the same time, then I thought, really ... it really makes you think twice. It's like six years on the course and its going to end up £20,000 in debt." (Jessie, 'dropout')

On top of student loans, many interviewees had found it necessary to take out other debts, such as bank overdrafts and credit cards. Although usually much smaller in amount, these were regarded more seriously than student loans, which were often used to repay these other loans, as were any wages from paid work.

> "Your student loans you've got to pay back, like, once you've finished, and then like you've got your overdraft as well because, like, sometimes your loan, I mean, like, my loan, doesn't cover everything. It's for travelling expenses – my loan this year is not enough to cover my books and all my travelling expenses.... Just when the next student loan comes in, I pay off the overdraft. It's like a vicious circle though." (Noreeen, 'straight-to-Degree')

Again, disadvantaged students faced a dilemma. In this instance, between taking on extra paid work to minimise debt, or taking out more debt to maximise study time.

> "I've cleared my overdraft now with my second instalment of my loan and working as well. So I was working quite a lot over Christmas and New Year, but that's sort of eating into my studying. But just trying to keep above ... just keeping above the overdraft, 'cos I know it's quite easy now to get £3,000 or £4,000 overdrafts, but I know I'm in debt already, so I'm trying no tae go that way as well." (Dorothy, 'progresser')

As time passed interviewees had come to terms with the necessity of debt, of all kinds, and were determined to complete their studentship no matter what the cost.

> "I wish I had applied for more loans – more money – because I'm in debt now, and I may as well just have took advantage of what I could have got before. Because before I didn't take out my maximum loan, and I was struggling the year before last year, and I wish I did take out the maximum loan, 'cos it would have helped me a lot.... I was resistant to getting more debt, but now I'm just, 'bugger it' – I might as well go." (Fergus, 'straight-to-Degree')

This attitude appeared to be related to a greater level of confidence about both dealing with money in the present and in the future, through a greater perceived likelihood of academic success leading to a higher paid job after graduation.

> "I tend not to worry about money, but I should because I'm really skint and I know that I'll be in lots of debt. But my idea is

the Degree that I'm doing and the job that I want to get at the end of the Degree will pay it back.... It [loan] would have worried me at the start, but and I've also got credit cards which I never dreamed of getting before. Well, I'll pay it off once I've got a job." (Malcolm, 'straight-to-Degree')

Student finance policy

Debt in this research was primarily due to respondents taking out student loans to finance their careers. This is different to what would have been experienced by previous generations of disadvantaged higher education students, who would have principally relied on student grants. The universal student grant was gradually phased out, to be replaced by loans, during the 1990s, and had completely disappeared at the time these young people were making their UCAS applications. Their financial situation was made more difficult by the introduction of student tuition fees at that time. Interviewees felt aggrieved that they were among the first to have suffered under the full force of these changes, which were felt to have reduced participation at all levels.

"I think taking away this grant put people off, you know, there was grants available, you know, and now there is really none. I mean that put me off, I mean, that was the just the year before I went to uni and it was, 'Oh my goodness what am I going to do?'." (Kayley, 'straight-to-Degree')

This was just one several aspects of current student finance policy with which interviewees were unhappy. Another concerned the apparent disparity between the FE and HE sectors, even within some institutions. Higher education students felt discriminated against, in that their friends studying certain FE courses were being paid non-repayable bursaries (as was also the case with nursing students).

"The thing about people who are still at college and still getting like bursaries and grants and stuff. I don't see why ... if they can still do it for them...? I know it is a big expense, but why is it so different for uni?" (Cecilia, 'straight-to-Degree')

"If the student loans became grants it would be fine, and it wouldn't need to be £3,000 just even £1,000 would be a difference. And I don't know how the college people just can bum about in high school and come down here and do Highers and get paid £220 a month, because that would pay my rent and would make me a lot happier." (Donald, 'straight-to-Degree')

One of the recommendations of the 1999 Cubie Inquiry for the Scottish Parliament into student finance was that some form of non-repayable bursary should be reintroduced to assist disadvantaged students. Unlike other recommendations by that inquiry, interviewees felt that this was a positive step, although, yet again, they felt that their age group had missed out, as the first students to receive this 'Young Student's Access Bursary' would be those who started in 2001-02.[1]

"I think the new system they are introducing in Scotland with bringing in grants and the endowment, I think that's a really good way because they have to cover their tuition fees somehow. I think that's really good – they should put it across the whole of Britain. I'm very annoyed that I will miss the student grants when they start this year, but because I went last year I won't get them, which I don't think is fair.... If I'd left it another year I could have gone to uni and not owed any money, and now I owe £15,000." (Elspeth, 'deferrer')

"This year my wee brother went to college and he didn't have to take out such a big loan, because you get a Young Student's Bursary and I was raging. I was like, 'Oh I hate you', 'cos he only ended up with like a £500 loan and he got the other £600 in bursary, and I think that's quite a good idea." (Annie, 'restart')

The main recommendation of the Cubie Inquiry was that the recently introduced student tuition fees should be paid in arrears in Scotland, rather than in advance as in the rest of the UK. Interviewees were less enthusiastic about the

---

[1] The Young Student's Access Bursary, introduced by the Scottish Parliament for new students starting in 2001-02, provides £2,000 per year for young people whose parents' combined income is less than £10,000 per year.

abolition of up-front tuition fees, as, owing to their disadvantage, many in this research would not have been eligible to pay *any* fees under the old system, others only a small amount.

> "I'd reintroduce the grants for a start, but that's about it. I don't actually care about the tuition fee that doesn't affect me." (Johnny, 'straight-to Degree')

The other side of the coin to the abolition of up-front tuition fees was their proposed replacement by a system of payment in arrears, called the 'Graduate Endowment Payment'. The introduction of this policy had left some interviewees in a state of uncertainty, regarding what they would have to pay and when.[2]

> "This is one I'm very unsure of because in first year I had to pay a contribution – it was £44 or something – which was strange in itself because my brother was still at university at that point and he didn't have to, and it was based on the same parents' income. But since there's been the Cubie Report and everything, I'm very unsure of what the position actually is now and whether I now will have to pay when I finish or.... And everyone I've asked seems to have a different version of how it will actually work out – no one seems to actually know.... Yeah, under the old system I was a lot better off." (Colleen, 'straight-to-Degree')

Predictably, those who had worked out that this new system penalised disadvantaged students such as themselves were angry, especially as this was seen as an extra debt that they had not had the opportunity to take into account at the start of their student career.

> "Do you know if I'm paying this £2,000 at the end of the Degree? I wasn't paying tuition fees, 'cos my mum and dad wernae earning that much – over the barrier or whatever. But I don't know if I have to pay it or not, but if I have to pay it, I'm not looking forward to that – two grand down the tubes." (Donald, 'straight-to-Degree')

---

[2] The Graduate Endowment Payment is a one-off £2,000 charge, which all young people, including those from the most disadvantaged backgrounds, will have to meet once their earnings exceed £10,000 per year.

> "I hope to God that they don't do *that*! [Graduate Endowment tax] [...] It's obviously better for people who had to pay fees, but for people who probably don't have to pay fees...?" (Christel, 'straight-to-Degree')

One group of disadvantaged interviewees were still having to pay tuition fees in advance, specifically those who were repeating a year of study (for non-medical reasons). For example, this interviewee blamed repeating on having previously taken on two jobs, which ironically she now needed even more to cover her fees.

> "I done the two [jobs in a shop and a restaurant] for a while, but wae the fees, I couldnae give any of them up. I was considering giving one of them up this year, but I cannae ... because that was one of the reasons, problems, I failed last year – I was working too much and I didn't have time to study.... Aye, how do I pay and study at the same time?" (Charlotte, 'repeater')

For the disadvantaged, being told that they were now eligible to pay for their tuition (as well as another year's debt) was an unexpected and serious obstacle, which compounded their existing difficulties, leading to further reduced participation.

> "I couldn't get finance for the second year, because I was still going into my first year again.... Basically, that meant that they wanted £1,000 off me for this year and I went to student services and all they could come up with was the direct debit of £177 per month, which on a part-time job [Pizza Hut] and going to uni as well it would just be too expensive." (George, 'dropout')

> "I thought I would maybe be able to pay my tuition fees if I was working all the time, but it just never worked out that way, and I was getting quite tired, like – skipping lectures to get home and sleep, basically." (Sheena, 'repeater')

Another way in which having to repeat a year of study could become a blow for disadvantaged students was that this could result in the loss of income from any scholarships. This setback also applied to those who became 'restarts'.

"Last year I found it hard because I didn't get a scholarship, because I went back to doing a first year again. So I didnae have it last year and last year it was terrible."
(Annie, 'restart')

Those who were (still) in receipt of scholarships had found this to have had a positive effect on their student life. Predictably, most interviewees felt that a non-repayable grant system of student funding *for all* should be reintroduced to widen participation. In the end, it was felt that contemporary student finance policy did little to help young people from similar backgrounds to themselves to be successful in higher education.

"I'd make it free. I don't know, that's about it. That's the only bad point – the money situation. I mean, there's a lot of folk that could go to uni but cannac go 'cos they've no' got the money to go." (Laurie, 'straight-to-Degree')

"I really wanted to have a great a job and the great career and the great house and the great big family and all things that you kind of feel as if your mum and dad missed out on, and you didn't have as a child."
(Loretta, 'dropout')

"What would you say was the main reason that you left early?" (interviewer)

"Just the money – to me it was the money."
(Loretta)

Cultural disadvantage

Non-academic background

It might be argued that a lack of preparedness to take on the financial burden of a full-time studentship was one of a number of more subtle aspects of interviewees' disadvantage. Many came from family backgrounds in which both taking on debt to invest in one's future and participation in higher education were alien concepts. In such families, historically, children had left school to get a job and contribute to family income. Indeed, some interviewees felt aware of some pressure from their families and friends to do likewise.

"At their [parents'] time, there wasn't a lot of university courses, it was you go get a job, you work hard. And they're all working class and I'm working class as well, so to understand their position, so when they don't see you, when you're reading a book, they get the idea that maybe 'let's chase him'." (Callum, 'returner')

"They [family] think that it's really hard to find a job at the end so what's the point in doing four years if you're maybe not going to get something at the end. Because you could have worked and maybe climbed yourself up the ladder already." (Chin-Ho, 'progresser')

As always, this barrier seemed to exert the greatest influence on interviewees attempting more advanced or prestigious courses.

"Philosophy is something that I've always been interested in, but I've never told anybody, you know, because they get this sort of idea, you know where they go, 'huh?' But it is a lot of fun ... I'm a kid from the East End and when I say that I want to do Law, people think, 'Christ, you must be from Bearsden [a 'posh' suburb]', or something like." (Callum, 'returner')

"I tend to lie quite a lot. Like, if I am out on a night and people ask you what you do, I'll just say that I am a student. And my friends – a lot of them are engineers – so if I'm out with them I'll just kind of go, like, nod when they are saying that they are engineers.... Just in town [central Glasgow], I think I like the town, because I look on upon myself as I've got more in common with the people. I think if I don't say that I'm a medical student then they'll get a better idea of what kind of person I am."
(Ellen, 'straight-to-Degree')

If an attitude of 'inverse snobbery' was also held by the interviewees themselves, this could lead to reduced participation, particularly if the more attractive alternative of a working identity was on offer.

"I didn't like being a student at all.... I couldn't put my finger on any one thing, it's just wee bits. I didn't like the studying; I didn't like the not having enough money all the time; didn't like ... I don't know. However, I liked the college itself and I liked the people that were there, I just didn't like the lifestyle.... I just got offered that job as a rough-caster and I just took it.... More money. I don't like sitting about, I don't like office jobs or anything like that; I prefer being out ... out in the open." (Sammy, 'dropout')

It was felt that this 'worker ethos' exerted a greater influence over males, particularly in ex-industrial (and disadvantaged) areas, which offered few opportunities for graduate-based employment and more unskilled or manual (and male-oriented) jobs.

"All the, just, boys seem to have stayed [in remote area], there is quite a lot of jobs like joiners, mechanics and things like that, but nothing for girls apart from a shop or an office." (Elspeth, 'deferrer')

"I know people who, like, who didn't go to uni and they're working in call-centres full-time and I think, 'no I couldn't do that every day'.... It's really more guys I know – they've ended up in call-centres and I just think they're not going to be ... it's alright now, they make more money than everyone, but not in the end." (Vivian, 'dropout')

This 'anti-education' culture may be one reason why the majority of respondents in this research were female and also why the females in this project were less likely to finish the project as 'never-students'.

"I think it's better for the females than males though, I think that the guys had a harder time than us.... They'd get called poofs and stuff if they were *at all* interested in class." (Ellen, 'straight-to-Degree')

Perceptions of higher education

Even among those who did value higher education, some of the attitudes and values of their non-academic backgrounds appeared to hamper their careers in higher education. For example, despite their distractions, the pull of family and friends was often cited as a reason for not leaving home or not enrolling in far-off institutions. This indicates that a proportion of the respondents who chose to stay at home and travel to their nearest institution may have done so for cultural, as well as economic, reasons. This may, in turn, be a reason why those who did not leave home or who travelled to a nearby institution were more likely to reduce their level of participation (see Chapter 4).

"I picked this uni [Glasgow] just because, well, the only real options were this and Strathclyde [also located in Glasgow], and I knew quite a few people from my school were coming here, plus it's nearer.... I've got a girlfriend and I'm happy just staying at home. I don't have to pay nothing and I've got a couple of part-time jobs and stuff." (Rab, 'straight-to-Degree')

"I never really thought I was ready, I mean, I was like seventeen or eighteen and, in fairness, I just wanted to go where my pals were and stuff like that. I had no concept of what I was going to do, so I just felt, keep it in Glasgow – close to the family and stuff like that." (Callum, 'returner')

Lack of confidence about one's abilities to cope with independent living, away from family and friends, was just one of a range of interrelated psychological barriers which had hindered the progress of many of those interviewed. For example, this reticence about leaving home could be compounded in the minds of some respondents by low academic aspirations, feelings of financial insecurity, uncertainties about student life, poor future expectations and a more general underlying lack of confidence.

"I was eighteen or whatever and I didnae really want to leave, but I thought Calley ['new' university] is just one bus run out the road and all.... Really I didnae just want to leave my parents. I didnae know if I would be able to kind of cope at this, you know what I mean? I wanted to stay under my own [that is, parental] roof." (Ben, 'straight-to-Degree')

"It's too far away [English or Edinburgh institutions]. You would have to, like, spend a lot of money, plus you're not guaranteed you are going to get something out of the course for it." (Chin-Ho, 'progresser')

In the extreme, this unwillingness to leave home could even cost a place at university, such as in the case of this respondent who was only accepted at a far-off institution offering the Degree course that she had spent a year at FE college to qualify for.

> "I visited the one in Dundee ['red brick' university] and I preferred the one in Dundee, atmosphere-wise kind of thing, but then that would have meant having to move.... I'm a wimp – I found it a bit scary. I really hadn't got a clue about anything about it. I wouldn't know where to start about getting accommodation or anything like that." (Kathleen, 'completer')

Interviewees who lived in the remote study area *had* to leave home if they wanted to participate in higher education. Being forced to move away could also have negative consequences for insecure young people, such as this interviewee who became homesick and unhappy with student life, resulting in her dropping out.

> I just wasn't happy. I was getting on fine – I passed all the exams that I sat so far. I just wasn't happy.... I didn't like the halls; I didn't really like student life at all. I don't think I'm cut out to be a party animal ... I was very homesick." (Kirsten, 'dropout')

Other interviewees displayed a lack of confidence about the 'big step' of moving from school to higher education itself.

> "I wished I got through last year when I was supposed to, but I feel that I am prepared for it this year. I didn't really feel that I was going to be able to get through last year – I just didn't feel assured of myself enough.... I just didn't feel confident enough to make it." (Jock 'repeater')

> "I thought it was like a big jump goan fae school straight intae uni. I thought it was too much o' a jump." (Lizzie, 'progresser')

Lizzie's comment is a feeling that was held by many interviewees, which, in her case, had led to her choosing to enrol in a HND course at an FE college for two years before progressing to a university Degree. As is elaborated on later, in hindsight, some young people who had made

this choice regretted it. Worse still, this lack of confidence, coupled with prior misconceptions of universities entrance criteria, could result in interviewees becoming students at an institution below their optimal level.

> "I was doing the HND. Before I left school I didn't realise I was going to come away with as many Highers as I did, so I just applied – I didn't apply for any university courses, I just applied for college. And so once I got there and I realised that I had enough Highers to get me into a university course, I didn't really have as much heart in it [HND] as I thought I would, so I just sort of left at that." (Eleanor, 'returner' [now studying a Degree course])

> "Nothing put me off going to Glasgow ['ivy league'] at all. It's just I didn't think I would get the grades to get in, but unfortunately I did. So if I had believed in myself I would probably be a student in Glasgow." (Audrey, 'straight-to Degree' [accessed Strathclyde 'red brick'])

Institutional 'habitus'

Like so many other barriers, the psychological barriers faced by interviewees appeared to be greatest among those who were contemplating the most advanced or prestigious courses. The perception of some interviewees that their optimal institution was 'elitist' could actually act as a barrier to increased participation.

> "See because they've [art school, HE college] got such a big name, and it's like, oh you've got to be great to get in there and all that, it puts a lot of pressure on you. I was asked to go for an interview and I was absolutely terrified – I nearly got ran over going to it, I was that worried. I suppose they are known ... people will say that they are very snobby." (Kathleen, 'completer')

Others had decided from the outset against applying for more prestigious institutions (such as 'ivy league' universities) for non-academic reasons.

> "Glasgow ['ivy league'] had sort of a stern appearance. Strathclyde ['red brick'] – they

had more emphasis on the counselling services available, they're supportive, and Glasgow didn't have the reputation for being very supportive – sorry!" (Christel, 'straight-to-Degree')

This view often persisted or was even reinforced among those who did enrol in such institutions. Feeling culturally 'at odds' with such institutions or their staff had clear repercussions for commitment to continued participation.

"You feel much more, like, on your own at [Glasgow, 'ivy league'] university, there's no … I wouldn't say that there is one member of staff that I would ever talk to or turn to." (Ellen, 'straight-to-Degree')

"I think that when you do approach them [at Glasgow], they are so intelligent in a way that they don't know how to respond to your questions in simple terms. So there is no point in going to see them because it doesn't help you…. I've got quite a lot of friends at Calley [Caledonian, 'new' university] and they say that the whole class is smaller, so it's more personalised. You sort of know your lecturer more – he'll probably know your name – and I think that would make it easier to go and see him. And what from what I've heard the lecturers are younger and more helpful." (Rab, 'straight-to Degree')

Interestingly, although this problem was mentioned at all levels (between HE and FE), 'ivy league' universities were seen as particularly aloof. This was borne out by those who had switched from 'ivy league' to other types of institution.

"One thing I never did was go for help when I had a problem and I think that they could be a wee bit more forthcoming [at Glasgow]…. They seemed a wee bit more forthcoming [at Caledonian]. In their lectures, they always said, this is my door, it's always open, you know where I am." (Evelyn, 'dropout')

"I like the system that they [Caledonian] work. If you're having troubles you can go and see your Head of Department without any problem and talk away to them. You always … I always, felt scared to go near

them at Glasgow [University] in case I got booted out or something like that. There's a lot of pressure there; there's a lot less pressure here; they are a lot easier going, you get a lot more help." (Jimmy, 'restart')

Such perceptions of being a 'fish out of water' at prestigious institutions were often compounded by issues relating to disadvantage, especially when their classmates often displayed greater levels of both economic and cultural capital.

"I was finding it a bit hard when I went away – I felt there was a big gap between me, I noticed, and everybody else. And there was all these people in my tutorial speaking, translating in Latin and Greek, and that was quite intimidating. My school only did Modern English." (Elspeth, 'deferrer')

"I find that the people … the people that I have came into contact with in lectures and tutorials tend to be from a different background…. It seems to be the people that I meet – maybe it is just me – are sort of more middle class, you know, and sort of have a southern English background, but it probably is just me. I just don't seem to fit into that aspect. There have been a couple of people just the same and we get on fine. Its just I think there is more … it's this university ['ivy league'] – bit of more middle class, it attracts more." (Archie, 'repeater')

With some interviewees, this could lead to the perception that any elitism, even discrimination, originated from their student peers, rather than their chosen institution.

"You want to enjoy your time at uni; you want to be able to talk to people without, you know, feeling, I don't want to open my mouth in class because they're gonnae hear my accent and know that I'm no coming fae, you know, somewhere like that. That's why I chose Caledonian, 'cos all the professors spoke like me, you know, they all had this kind of a voice, and everybody that went there, was just like me. There was nobody there you know walking aboot like aw' I'm too good for everybody else." (Evelyn, 'dropout')

"A lot of people I've spoke to are from private schools and if not then still very.... I don't feel inadequate, I just feel.... Yeah, well I think there is elitism. I would not say that they would look down, but I would just say there is that aspect.... Yeah, definitely comes from the students, I find." (Archie, 'repeater')

These negative experiences of higher education clearly have the potential to become self-reinforcing. The more non-standard students who discontinue ('dropout') or switch ('restart') from prestigious courses the more these will become perceived by the disadvantaged as 'elitist'. This may especially be the case when other, less prestigious, courses are not perceived as carrying the same baggage. Indeed, even those who had been successful in prestigious courses were unwilling to recommend them to others from schools in disadvantaged areas.

"I don't think that if you come from the East End that you fit in at Glasgow University, is always useful. I think that if you could do a course at Strathclyde University or somewhere, you are probably better doing that than coming here.... It's just everybody's ... it's just they've got a different background than you. They've got more money than you, which makes a big difference about where they go out. I mean, like, we had a ball there and I couldn't afford to go and everybody's like, 'how can you not go to this?' It's £35 a ticket; you have to buy a dress – everybody's going in these posh dresses – 'Oh, you must have at least a cocktail dress?', 'No, I don't really go places wi' cocktails', 'Well, what do you do when your family are going out?', 'Well my mum and dad don't go to places where I need a ball-gown'. So it's just a different world and I think it's easy for them because they are all together, but it is harder for them to understand your world." (Ellen, 'straight-to-Degree')

Encouraging others

Having spent time in post-school education, some interviewees were sufficiently positive about the advantages it could bring to feel able to encourage others from their background to do likewise.

"I'm trying to encourage my boyfriend to go just now because he is wanting to do an IT course.... Aye, it would be good for him because he actually left school when he was fourteen, so he's no' got a lot of qualifications, so if he goes and does an IT ... quite a lot of jobs in IT just now." (Lara, 'dropout')

A few interviewees had actually gone back to their schools to try to encourage others. It is perhaps a measure of how far they themselves had come that they were taken aback by the lack of enthusiasm which they encountered.

"When I went back and did that talk it was totally bizarre because no one was interested in anything that was outwith where they were." (Ailsa, 'deferrer')

"A lot of them thought it wasnae them. There was a few of them thought it was great and they could do anything they wanted.... I think they were just ... they didnae want to do everything theirselves; spend money on all the materials theirself – they wanted everything done for them." (Sinclair, 'repeater')

Interestingly, these experiences highlight the same issues that interviewees who had reduced participation raised themselves, namely, independent study, confidence, money and culture (fitting in). One interviewee felt that more such people could be tempted into higher education by stressing the aspects of being student that would be more attractive to their culture, rather than more traditional values.

"You just say to them to get out. Got to speak to them something that they understand. Say there is hundreds of birds up there, ken what I mean? It is a good experience; it gets you out of here; get student loans; massive amounts of money. As long as you do some studying you get hundreds of time to kick about, get steaming. Basically dae everything you dae the noo, dae a bit of studying and you will end up with a Degree one day." (Jock, 'repeater')

Career disadvantage

When to start

The previous study indicated that the above barriers could also deter qualified but disadvantaged young people from enrolling in higher education in the first place. These continued to influence those who had initially deferred making an application.

"I mean, my boyfriend didn't want me to come to college ... but I was like, 'naw, I'm going'. He didn't want to be going out with a student. Aye, he's like that, 'you're going to turn into a freak'." (Libby, 'deferrer')

Most interviewees who had taken a 'gap year' to work and save for their studentship spoke positively of this route in terms of it preparing them for independent living, budgeting their finances, getting all the 'partying out their system', allowing them time to decide what they wanted to do with their lives and to choose the right course.

"I think a lot of people, I think, are pressurised as soon as you leave school. I had it in my head as well – if you didn't go straight to college or straight to university then that was it, it's a failure, you know what I mean? But I definitely recommend going out ... a lot of people I speak to don't really know what they want to do when they leave school – are confused and don't know what they want. But, aye, after me taking time out and actually living in the 'real working world' [patronising voice] and that, I've realised where I want to go with it, you know. So I feel a lot more, I don't know, I just want to get on with it now – I'm looking forward to doing the course." (Eleanor, 'returner')

"I saved up when I was working in my year out. I saved up. I managed to save quite a bit of money, because I was working three jobs actually at the time, and so I saved up a bit of money and then I got my [full] loan and I went back last summer and worked in 'Eileanbeg' [remote area]. So I managed to actually get myself out my overdraft. But, em, that's really the only money problem, is

getting really close to my overdraft limit...." (Lucy, 'deferrer')

However, a number of potential disadvantages to this strategy were also identified, the most obvious being that, in terms of education, a 'year out' effectively reduces participation by putting such students a 'year behind' and out of practice at studying.

"I was bit worried when I went away [to university] about essays because I hadn't written for a year and a half, but it's fine.... The first one for my English wasn't so good, but after that I think...." (Elspeth, 'deferrer')

Such interviewees could also have become accustomed to working and earning. This could amplify the deterrent effect of the prospect of debt or create financial stress.

"Having a wage and come back off and actually having loans, that is pretty heavy. You always run out of money near the end of term." (Gregor, 'deferrer')

These same issues resurfaced with interviewees who had already left a previous course. For disadvantaged 'completers' and 'dropouts', who were considering becoming 'returners', there was now the added deterrent of their past negative experiences with higher education, especially outstanding debts.

"Make it more accessible for people from low-income families, because I think that's maybe the thing that would put people off. It puts me off going back now because I don't think that I could afford it – I'd have to somehow save up lots of money, take out another loan." (Jessie, 'dropout')

Which route to take

During this research, a number of pathways through or towards higher education were identified. Although 'straight-to-Degree' was the desired route by most, others decided on a more gradual strategy. There were two reasons for this. First, for those who had not attained sufficient Highers at school to access university directly, the FE college route could only bring educational benefits. This was true even for those who had left their school, in a disadvantaged area, with no Highers points at all.

"I'd tell them [at school] to consider college, because leaving school I didnae have qualifications, it is, and look at me now I'm at uni, it is. And at school I was eiwiz thought of, no' top of the class, but no' bottom, it is, and I'm at uni and there's folk that were top of the class that arenae even got this far." (Morven, 'progresser')

The second reason for some choosing the FE route was related to confidence and prior perceptions of more prestigious institutions (that is, the 'big step' referred to earlier).

"I wouldnae advise anybody to just come straight to uni after school. I think it's just so much easier this year because college did prepare me well enough, and the school didnae prepare me for college, so I don't think it'd prepare anybody for uni.... Uni's a step up fae college, but I'm finding it easier 'cos I've done all the background stuff.... I wouldnae have understood a thing in the first year and I would have just mucked up the rest." (Chad, 'progresser')

Those who decided on this gradual approach towards university found out later that it could have some drawbacks. First and foremost, as outlined in the previous chapter, for those who gained an HND, choices of university were not equitable. Specifically, only some universities (that is 'new' universities) offered direct entry into the third (Degree) year.

"I applied for direct entry to third year [at 'new' university], you know, because I didnae want to do another four years.... A Degree's a Degree – that's the way I see it. [...] When I finish the noo, I just want tae get a job." (Chad, 'progresser')

"It was first [year].... Yeah, I wasn't very happy about that but it was a better calibre of university ['ivy league'] than the other one so.... I could have gone to Paisley ['new' university], but I'm finding out now that if you do the first year of this course then you get into the fourth at Paisley and I'm thinking that's not that kind of Degree I'm wanting, so...." (Leonora, 'progresser')

The downside of enrolling at a more prestigious ('ivy league') institution was that this could mean at least an extra two years of study, which also meant the prospect of more loans and more forgone wages, as well any other institution-related costs. On top of all this, interviewees who had gone back into the first year of a higher education course could find that they were now eligible to pay tuition fees.

"At College I didn't have to pay them [fees], but because I'm going down a level, as it were, going intae first year, I had to pay it, but it was alright so that [Carnegie] trust paid it for me [her brother informed her].... I was totally freaking out about it, because I didn't realise that I had to pay my tuition fees for the first year, so I was like, 'Oh!'." (Leonora, 'progresser')

This was not the only problem encountered by those who had successfully attained a university place via this route. Such students also felt penalised because they were only awarded smaller loans for their final term in a Diploma course, even if they were due to advance to Degree level in the following October (supposedly because they could choose to leave with an HND and claim benefit). Others found that they had to pay for course materials (such as laptop computers) that students who had begun in the first year were given free by the university. In the end the prospect of these extra burdens could lead to Diplomates deciding against progressing to a university Degree course.

"I couldn't afford to move, not with already being two student loans while I was at college. I couldn't afford to go down there and stay in the halls or rent as well.... Money definitely – the money thing was first. It's like, I couldn't afford it. I did apply and got into unis in England and they sent me stuff on the accommodation and that and it's like I can't afford it, 'cos it'd be two years that I'd have to go down and thought, 'nut, I can't afford it'." (Patricia, 'completer')

How far to go

As stated earlier, some respondents had already left full-time education after completing a course of one or two years' duration (such as HNC or HND). Meanwhile, other students who had reached this point decided to stay on and progress to a more advanced qualification. Among those who had progressed to university, the lure of employment could still remain strong; indeed, it could become strengthened when already having a qualification was weighed up against the costs of progressing.

> "Maybe later on in life I will regret dropping out – I know I will. But it's just the fact that I have got an HND and I will get a job wi' my HND." (Lizzie, 'progresser')

Other Diplomates had been unable to find a job with their HND qualifications and had then, rather reluctantly, progressed to university.

> "I wiznae going tae come to the uni during the summer and I didn't make my mind up until late in September that I was coming. And then I'd been looking for a job all summer and all the jobs that I was interested in says, 'must be qualified to Degree level'." (Chad, 'progresser')

This mirrors a finding of the earlier study, outlined in Chapter 2, which indicated that some disadvantaged young people had only entered post-school education in the first place as 'reluctant students' because they had been unable to find employment on leaving school. This reluctance factor continued to be an issue, even to postgraduate level, which some would only consider if they could not find a job on graduation.

> "I think I'd go for a job – shout 'show me the money!' [...] Just that if there were nae jobs I would stay on and do the postgraduate." (Jock, 'repeater')

> "Well, for my placement year if I got offered ... if I just got my Degree, I didn't need Honours and they would give me a job once I left, then I would go, definitely." (Lucy, 'starter')

Lucy's dilemma was one currently facing most of those who had gone 'straight-to-Degree'. These students had now reached the point where they had to decide whether or not to continue on to an Honours (fourth) year at university or to complete their education after only three years of study with an Ordinary Degree. Once again, this dilemma involved making a painful cost–benefit analysis.

> "At the moment, at the end of this year I will have about £10,500 worth of debt. If I go on next year I'll probably be another £3,000 on top and they are charging about £16 a month interest which is no' much fun is it? If I didn't have to worry about the loans, I would probably go next year and just, considering I passed my exams this year, I'd just go next year and see what happens, but I can't guarantee that I will pass my exams next year and I don't know if I will come out with nothing apart from three grand worth of debt." (Johnny, 'straight-to Degree')

At the end of this research, almost two thirds of respondents were still in full-time education. Although at first glance this may seem a very positive situation, during face-to-face interviews it became clear that many were already contemplating when to discontinue their education. As always, it was those who were enrolled in the most prestigious (costly) courses who were being forced to make the greatest sacrifices.

> "I'd quite like to do an Integrated Degree – quite a lot of people are doing that. But there is no way I'd take out extra ... basically, you take a year out of Medicine and you do another Degree, but if you do a year you get Degree, if you do two you get an Honours Degree. And it means that when you qualify, because of the nature of our course, that it's not just the basic stuff; it means that you'd get a better job at the end of it. And they're advising this is the course to go on, and a lot – about half of the year's going off to do that, but there's no way I'm taking out an extra year or two years loans for it." (Ellen 'straight-to Degree')

> "I don't think I'm going to do Honours, 'cos I just want to kinda get my Degree, finish next year and then kinda start doing what I want to do.... It's two years – you have to go away abroad to study and I just can't afford it to be honest. And then coming back for a fifth year, it's just too much." (Annie, 'restart')

Many of the interviewees who had been successful academically, at school and in higher education, were now among the most eager to finish the experience.

"It's just a case of finishing – it's only another year after this. It's like *a sentence.* Like I was saying to you earlier, just get it out the way and that's it, you've got it.... Aye, if I had the choice, I'd have been home the first week, but I suppose you have to stick it out." (Donald, 'straight-to Degree')

"I think I just want to get qualified and start working and do that. I think I've lost a lot of the ambition that I had at school.... At school I was the best in a lot of my classes, or joint best, whereas now I feel like I'm the bottom of the heap." (Ellen, 'straight-to-Degree')

These negative opinions, especially among the most talented interviewees, appeared to be compounded by the view that the academic challenges presented by higher education were not as arduous as the socioeconomic barriers to be overcome.

"To be honest with you, I think uni has been a bit of a waste of time actually. I know I'm only doing it to get my Degree, but I wouldn't say that I've actually learned that much more than what I did when I was working." (Ailsa, 'deferrer')

"I didn't find the learning curve for learning as hard as the learning curve for money." (Fergus, 'straight-to-Degree')

Summary

By analysing face-to-face interviews with a cross-section of respondents, this chapter has examined some of the reasons why the young people in this project had taken the educational pathways detailed in previous chapters. In particular, it has focused on the reasons why some respondents had reduced their level of participation in higher education while others had not. A number of factors were found to be acting as barriers that influenced the decision-making processes of disadvantaged students. These barriers related to interviewees' educational, economic and cultural backgrounds. Many of these barriers were found to be very much interconnected and often compounded each other in ways that eventually resulted in reduced participation. Usually, no single issue was paramount in this decision-making process, which tended to involve weighing up the costs (for example, financial, psychological or the lure of employment) against the benefits of continuing in higher education. These same barriers were found to be operating at all levels, resulting in early completion, dropping-out and deciding to forego the opportunity to advance to Honours or postgraduate level. The young people in this research were often faced with the difficult decision of how far they would go in education before these barriers prevented them from progressing any further. Ultimately this meant that it was the most aspiring and talented disadvantaged young people, attempting the most advanced or prestigious qualifications, who were facing the greatest barriers.

6

Conclusions and policy implications

Widening access to higher education has been an issue of great policy relevance in the UK in recent years. Although the gap in representation between the most affluent and the most disadvantaged groups of young people entering post-school education has remained large, there has nevertheless been an increase in the number of new entrants from non-traditional student backgrounds. However, the inequity of interest in higher education between the affluent and disadvantaged has not been confined to the numbers entering. Recently, the disproportionate numbers of students from disadvantaged backgrounds who fail to complete their courses (or leave with inferior qualifications) has also become a salient policy issue. This research has endeavoured to uncover the reasons why such young people are experiencing a poorer level of success in higher education as compared with their more affluent peers.

From an earlier project (Forsyth and Furlong, 2000), on which this research has built, it was clear that underachievement at school was the main factor limiting access to higher education among disadvantaged young people. This pre-existing underachievement not only limited whether or not such young people were able to access higher education but it also governed the level of access gained (for example, in terms of qualification being studied). In other words, disadvantaged students were usually participating at a less advanced or prestigious level within post-school education from the outset of their student careers. This, in itself, partially explains why some disadvantaged students fail to achieve the highest qualifications and, conversely, why some less prestigious courses, subjects or institutions have larger numbers of students who leave prematurely. The current project examined why academically able but socioeconomically disadvantaged students discontinue their careers in higher education prematurely.

This project tracked the student careers of the disadvantaged school-leavers who participated in the previous project. As expected, many of the young people who took part had reduced their level of participation in post-school education, either by dropping-out or by early completion of their studies. Others, who until now had remained within full-time education, were considering doing likewise in the near future. Others were expecting to continue within full-time education, although sometimes reluctantly so, despite having experienced a range of difficulties and barriers that had restricted their progress. Using both quantitative and qualitative techniques, this research identified these barriers, which either alone or in combination could lead to a disadvantaged young person deciding to prematurely discontinue their student career.

Summary of findings

Among the first obstacles faced by students from disadvantaged backgrounds were various educational barriers inherited from their schooldays. The relative underachievement at school of young people from the most disadvantaged families (found to be present even within schools located in areas of deprivation) was a factor that continued to limit their careers within post-school education. This was particularly the case among non-Degree students. By the end of the project, some respondents now stated that they wished they had 'stuck in' more while at school. This prior underachievement seemed, at least in part, to be related to an anti-education culture, operating within schools that have disadvantaged catchments. This anti-education culture was seen as a particular problem among males, who may have been further influenced by the lure of unskilled (manual) jobs available within their local labour market. This situation was compounded by these local labour markets often being completely devoid of any graduate-based employment opportunities. Related to this issue, many respondents also mentioned prevalent low levels of educational aspirations. These were seen as operating not only within their local community in general, but also within their families and even within their secondary schools (among both pupils *and* staff). These lower aspirations were felt to limit the range of post-school opportunities on offer to those pupils who did value education, by pushing them toward more vocational courses and away from prestigious subjects or institutions. Further to this, some respondents, having now met young people from other backgrounds, felt that their schools had been relatively under-resourced, especially in terms of the meeting needs of the most aspiring or high achieving pupils.

A second type of obstacle inherited from respondents' schooldays concerned their lack of familiarity with higher education (courses, subjects, institutions and student life). Many of the most disadvantaged young people who took part in this research were the first from their families to have accessed higher education. As such, they had nobody in their family to give them any advice, such as on picking the right course or how to survive student finance polices. Young people in this position often sought out advice from their school guidance staff or careers service; however, this was often unsatisfactory, perhaps because the needs of the majority of non-achieving pupils at their schools were seen as more important. In schools at which most young people leave school at the minimum leaving age to directly enter the labour market, the young people who took part in this project could be viewed locally as 'success stories' who did not require any help or guidance. As a consequence of this lack of advice, many of the most talented young people who took part in this research ended up enrolling in unsuitable courses. This was found to be major factor in reducing participation by both the quantitative and qualitative methodologies used in this research.

Another set of obstacles relating to respondents' disadvantaged family backgrounds were, the more obvious, economic barriers. In short, these young people could not rely on their parents to fund their studentship, but had to rely on other sources of income, such as loans or paid work. Less obviously, this problem was compounded by disadvantaged students being much more wary of getting into debt in order to fund their studentship, as compared with even *relatively* more affluent peers (who may have had some form of financial safety net). In fact, fear of debt, rather actual amount of debt, was found to act as a barrier to continued participation. In contrast, those who were prepared to take on debt from the outset of their student careers were found to have fared better. Again, this pattern was found in both the quantitative and qualitative phases of the research. This apparent paradox may be as a result of some (more educationally aspiring or confident) disadvantaged young people being prepared to take on any amount of debt in order to obtain a Degree (when they expected to be able to pay it back), while other disadvantaged students (perhaps from family backgrounds particularly culturally averse to debt or unfamiliar with higher education and its potential benefits) were less willing to take out student loans. These students either could not afford to enter higher education in the first place or attempted to fund their studentship by other means, such as paid work, which could also hinder academic progress. As time passed, more respondents in this research began to see the necessity of debt in order to survive a full-time studentship. At this point they began to cut back on the amount of paid work they were involved with and took on extra debts, perhaps wishing that they had taken on more debt form the very start of their student career.

Another economic dilemma faced by disadvantaged students concerned travel and accommodation. Many students who took part in this research had enrolled at their nearest institution of higher education. This was partly a cost-cutting strategy (to have less travelling expenses or to retain part-time jobs), but was also related to their lack of familiarity with higher education institutions in general. In comparison with their more affluent peers, whose parents may pay for their term-time accommodation (without requiring their son or daughter to take on paid work), many of the most disadvantaged young people in this research felt obliged to stay at home and contribute to their parental household income (by using both paid work *and* student loans). Not only does living in the parental home limit the range of educational opportunities available for the prospective student, it also detracts from student life and hence commitment to continued study . Perhaps for these reasons, despite the obvious economic advantages of the 'stay-at-home' strategy, it was those students who did leave their parental home (and also those who travelled daily to more distant institutions) who were the more successful within post-school education.

Although some of the young people in this research stated that they felt they 'fitted in' better at university than they did in their home area, many disadvantaged young people felt that they had experienced difficulties adjusting to student life or the ('middle class') environment of their institution. Such feelings could present a serious deterrent to continued participation in higher education. This problem was found at all levels in the academic hierarchy, but was less of an issue among FE college students in comparison to university students. From both the quantitative and qualitative methods used in this research, it was clear that it was the most talented disadvantaged individuals, who had enrolled in prestigious Degree courses at 'ivy league' institutions, who were the most negatively influenced by this phenomenon. Disadvantaged young people in this situation could often feel like a 'fish out of water', with little in common with their new, more affluent, peers (both students *and* staff). A related issue, which often exacerbated feelings of cultural isolation, was the foregoing of a social life. A lack of spending money and a lack of free time (owing to the constraints of paid work and travel) were chiefly responsible for this. Ultimately this could lead to lowered morale and commitment to study, especially if both their now working, old (school) peers and their new, more affluent, classmates appeared to be enjoying a youthful social life. As with many of the other obstacles identified by this research project (such as involvement with paid work and remaining in the parental home), these social and cultural barriers could restrict the development of peer networking, integration into academic life and the formation of a student identity – all of which run counter to a successful career in higher education.

The various barriers facing disadvantaged students, uncovered by this research, were found to be very much interconnected. For example, choosing the wrong course – whether through poor guidance by schools or lack of family experience in HE or FE – could, in turn, lead to the student feeling culturally isolated. By themselves, such issues may not be sufficient to make a disadvantaged student decide to prematurely discontinue their academic career, but coupled with student hardship, the lack of social life and (the fear) of rising debt with no guarantee of job at the end of it, may, on balance, make discontinuing seem like the less painful option. Other than those relating to prior (school) underachievement, all of the barriers uncovered by this research were found to be greatest for those young people who were both the most talented *and* the most disadvantaged. For example, those from particularly disadvantaged backgrounds who had initially enrolled in the most advanced courses or subjects at the prestigious institutions, tended to face the greatest levels of academic unfamiliarity, economic hardship (such as course-related costs, travel or accommodation) and cultural isolation. With the passage of time, as more disadvantaged young people discontinue their student careers, those who do attempt to continue within higher education are likely to come up against these barriers with ever-increasing magnitude (such as rising debt, less time for paid work, fewer like-minded peers). These processes are likely to continue beyond (Degree) graduation, when disadvantaged students may be the most likely to be deterred from postgraduate study.

Recommendations

From the findings of this project, there are clearly a number of policy issues, which need to be addressed if the level of participation in higher education by disadvantaged young people is to be improved. It is concluded that many of the difficulties encountered by the young people in this research originate from their schooldays. As well as the general need to raise aspirations and improve qualifications, perhaps through the provision of more advanced teaching at schools located in deprived areas, it is recommended that a greater level of information about higher education in general be provided at this stage. It was of great concern that poor quality of information and guidance received at school was reported as having resulted in some disadvantaged young people being deterred from participation in higher education in the first place and in others becoming enrolled in the 'wrong' courses. The UCAS class, in which some felt they had their whole future decided for them within half an hour with minimal help, was highlighted as a particular cause for concern. The need to familiarise potential students in their two final school years with all aspects student life, such as time management, teaching methods, independent study and living, rather than just concentrating on the more academic aspects of a studentship, also needs to be addressed within such schools. These concerns must be seen as particularly important to young people who have no family history of higher education.

In order to address these problems, there is clearly a need to raise aspirations among pupils from disadvantaged areas from an early stage in secondary school. By the time this research commenced most pupils from such schools had already left full-time education. Early contact with academic institutions could help raise such schools' retention rates but, equally importantly for young people such as those who took part in this research, it could also help familiarise the minority of already aspiring pupils with academia. In the final two years, especially in the period prior to the UCAS class, we recommend that schools serving areas of disadvantage concentrate on this familiarisation process to ensure that their most successful pupils enrol in suitable higher education courses. Perhaps this could be achieved by taking such pupils out of class at this time, running ('away-day') visits to a variety of institutions and involving outsiders, such as student former pupils (including those who have been less than successful), university staff (such as mentors) and the guidance staff from other schools that have a high number of leavers enrolling in higher education. In schools in which there are particularly few high-achieving pupils, perhaps these goals could be achieved by pooling resources with other schools in a similar situation. This latter measure would also allow the young people involved to meet others with similar aspirations to themselves, which might help boost their confidence and reduce feelings of isolation.

As expected, many of the young people in who took part in this research were found to be (already) suffering a range of economic hardships. Those in further education who could not access student loans often felt their bursaries were inadequate, while those in higher education were jealous of these bursaries because of their dislike of the student loan system. As things stand, many disadvantaged students spent their student income (loan or bursary) on surviving (rent, travel, bills, food and so on) rather than on study materials or student life. It is concluded that providing disadvantaged students with additional funds could also combat some of the other barriers that adversely effect their level of participation in higher education. In particular, extra financial help could reduce dependency on term-time jobs and increase the numbers who can afford student accommodation. At present, relative to other students in higher education, those from disadvantaged backgrounds are handicapped by the long hours they spend in paid employment (when they can find some) or spend travelling, instead of spending these studying. We also, recommend that any extra financial assistance, such as non-repayable bursaries targeted at disadvantaged school-leavers, be weighted more towards those entering the longer more prestigious courses. At present, disadvantaged young people are deterred from enrolling in longer courses because of the extra years' of debt involved, the financial penalties incurred when progressing into such courses via an HND (such as smaller loans and tuition fees), the extra costs of course materials, the less 'free' time available to engage in paid work and the greater likelihood of having to leave the parental home to access such courses in the first place. From this research, it would appear that current student finance policy tends to push the most talented disadvantaged school-leavers towards courses well below their full academic potential.

As well the prohibitive costs involved, the large number of respondents in this research who were 'stay-at-home students' was also found to be related to a lack of confidence and other cultural factors. Clearly there is a need to instil a greater valuation of post-school education within disadvantaged communities. Some young people who took part in this research were unhappy with student life, either through feeling that they did not 'fit in' with their more 'middle class' student peers or through feeling that they would be happier in a (non-academic) job. Countering this is obviously a more difficult task than improving the provision (and targeting) of information or funding aimed at disadvantaged young people. Perhaps only increased graduate-based employment in their local areas could break this cycle. At present, it is those with the greatest potential talent, from the most disadvantaged backgrounds who face the greatest barriers to their advancement. Ultimately, the end product of such students leaving higher education prematurely is that their disadvantage will be transmitted to the next generation of young people from their background. With increasing numbers of young people from all social backgrounds now entering post-school education these inequalities need to be addressed, otherwise, on the evidence of this report, they are likely to become more intensified in the future.

Bibliography

Barke, M., Braidford, P., Houston, M., Hunt, A., Lincoln, I., Morphet, C., Stone, I. and Walker, A. (2000) *Students in the labour market: Nature, extent and implications of term-time employment among University of Northumbria undergraduates*, Research Report 215, London: DfEE.

Callender, C. and Kemp, V. (2000) *Changing student finances: Income, expenditure and the take up of student loans among full- and part-time higher education students in 1998/9*, Research Report 213, London: DfEE.

Carstairs, V. and Morris, R. (1991) *Deprivation and health in Scotland*, Aberdeen: Aberdeen University Press.

Dearing, R. (1997) *The National Committee of Inquiry into Higher Education*, London: The Stationery Office.

Forsyth, A.J.M. and Furlong, A. (2000) *Socioeconomic disadvantage and access to higher education*, Bristol/York: The Policy Press/Joseph Rowntree Foundation.

HM Inspectors of Schools (1997) *Leaver destinations from Scottish secondary schools 1994/95 to 1996/97*, Edinburgh: The Scottish Office.

Independent Committee of Inquiry into Student Finance (1999) *Student finance: Fairness for the future*, Edinburgh: Scottish Parliament.

Kennedy, H. (1997) *Learning works: Widening participation in further [education?]*, London: Further Education Council.

Lynch, K. and O'Riordan, C. (1998) 'Inequality in higher education: a study of class barriers', *British Journal of Sociology of Education*, vol 19, no 4, pp 445-79.

McLoone, P. (1994) *Carstairs scores for Scottish postcode sectors from the 1991 Census*, Glasgow: Public Health Research Unit, University of Glasgow.

Scottish Office (1997) *Further education in Scotland: Report by the Secretary of State for Scotland*, London: The Stationery Office.

Tinklin, T. and Raffe, D. (1999) *Entrants to higher education*, Edinburgh: Centre for Educational Psychology, University of Edinburgh.

UCAS (University and Colleges Admissions Service) (1999) *Statistical bulletin: Widening participation*, Cheltenham: UCAS.

Appendices

Appendix A: 'Baseline' sample demographics

	n	(%)		n	(%)
Sample size	395	(100)	Female 236	(59.7)	
Glasgow (city)	119	(30.1)	Ayr (small towns)	99	(25.1)
Lanark (large towns)	116	(29.4)	Argyll (remote areas)	61	(15.4)
Single parent	110	(28.2)	Only child	29	(7.3)
Mother unemployed	33	(8.4)	Mother works (full-time)	150	(38.2)
Father unemployed	33	(8.5)	Father works (full-time)	272	(70.3)
Deprived DEPCAT	288	(72.9)	*Manual Social Class[a]*	173	(50.3)
DEPCAT 1	0	(0)	Class I	25	(7.3)
DEPCAT 2	8	(2.0)	Class II	101	(29.4)
DEPCAT 3	22	(5.6)	Class IIIN	45	(13.1)
DEPCAT 4	77	(19.5)	Class IIIM	98	(28.5)
DEPCAT 5	127	(32.2)	Class IV	54	(15.7)
DEPCAT 6	99	(25.1)	Class V	21	(6.1)
DEPCAT 7	62	(15.7)	No occupation given	51	(–)
Category F ('Striving' ACORN) neighbourhood type (> 38)				220	(55.7)
Parental home within a Social Inclusion Partnership area (SIP)				167	(42.3)

Notes: The figures refer to data collected while respondents were at school in spring 1999.

[a] Social class percentages exclude the 12.9% respondents who could not provide a parental occupation.

	n	(%)		n	(%)
Lives in parental home	2,958	(75.1)	Lives in halls of residence	63	(16.0)
Lives in student flat	5	(2.0)	Lives in private rented flat	15	(3.8)
Council tenant	5	(1.3)	Owner occupier	2	(0.5)
Other	5	(1.3)			
Full use of a car	112	(28.9)	Occasional car access	58	(14.9)
Income from family	143	(39.0)	Income from work	223	(58.8)
Income from bursary	72	(18.8)	Other income	25	(6.6)
Income from loan	148	(39.6)			

Note: The figures refer to data collected during the baseline postal survey of October 1999.

Appendix B: Regression equations

Regression 1

Dependent variable	Adjusted R^2	F	p	Independent variables	t	p
Highers points	0.114	13.634	0.000	Social class	3.858	0.000
				Unclassifiable	-3.412	0.001
				Remote area	2.946	0.004
				Family HE/FE	2.504	0.019

Regression 2

Dependent variable	Adjusted R^2	F	p	Independent variables	t	p
Access level	0.412	138.873	0.000	Highers points	16.218	0.000
				DEPCAT	-2.271	0.024

Regression 3

Dependent variable	Adjusted R^2	F	p	Independent variables	t	p
Participation	0.069	10.712	0.000	Highers points	3.922	0.000
				DEPCAT	-2.968	0.003
				Small town	2.504	0.019

Regression 4

Dependent variable	Adjusted R^2	F	p	Independent variables	t	p
Academic success (all respondents)	0.525	85.676	0.000	Baseline success	9.771	0.000
				Highers points	4.685	0.000
				Family HE/FE	3.183	0.032
				Female gender	2.113	0.035

Regression 5

Dependent variable	Adjusted R^2	F	p	Independent variables	t	p
Academic success (all baseline students)	0.428	22.854	0.000	Baseline success	6.076	0.000
				Highers points	3.331	0.001
				'Other' loans	-2.864	0.005
				Anticipated debt	-2.831	0.005
				Student loans	2.728	0.007
				Left home	2.680	0.008
				Family HE/FE	2.501	0.013

Regression 6

Dependent variable	Adjusted R^2	F	p	Independent variables	t	p
Academic success (baseline Degree students only)	0.354	10.983	0.000	Baseline success	5.216	0.000
				'Other' loans	-3.386	0.001
				Social class	3.328	0.001
				First choice course	3.187	0.002
				'Other' funds	3.073	0.003
				Bursary pupil	-2.272	0.025
				Student loans	2.178	0.030
				Travel time	2.128	0.035

Regression 7

Dependent variable	Adjusted R^2	F	p	Independent variables	t	p
'Straight-to-Degree'	0.123	6.131	0.000	'New' university	-3.201	0.001
				'Ivy league' university	-2.751	0.007
				Taken out loan	2.568	0.011
				'Other' loans	-2.532	0.012

Notes

Variables used in all above regression equations were: Highers points, gender, (parental) social class, 'unclassified' social class, being from a single-parent family, parents' work status, car access, a measure of happiness, having been a bursary pupil while at school, having a family member who had been in post-school education (FE or HE), DEPCAT, ACORN, SIP area, and if from Glasgow (city study area), Lanarkshire (large town), Ayrshire (small town) or Argyll (remote area).

Student variables used in Regressions 5, 6 and 7 (only) were: if left parental home, fees paid, unconditional offer, if in first choice course, if at first choice institution, if at nearest institution, type of university (Regression 7 only), proportion of friends at same institution, travel time to institution, cost of daily travel, time spent in paid work, if work clashes with study, any debt, total debt, anticipated final debt, total income, if any income from family, from work, from loans, from bursaries or from parents and expected importance of income from parents, from bursaries, from 'other' funds (eg scholarships), from student loans, from 'other' loans (eg bank), from paid work or from 'extra income' (eg 'fiddling') during student career.

Appendix C: 'Final' sample demographics

	n	(%)		*n*	(%)
Sample size	308	(100)	Female 186		(60.4)
Glasgow (city)	81	(26.3)	Ayr (small towns)	85	(27.6)
Lanark (large towns)	89	(28.9)	Argyll (remote areas)	53	(17.2)
Single parent	83	(27.4)	Only child	23	(7.5)
Mother unemployed	21	(6.9)	Mother works (full-time)	116	(37.8)
Father unemployed	27	(8.9)	Father works (full-time)	214	(70.4)
Deprived DEPCAT	216	(70.1)	*Manual Social Class*[a]	131	(48.5)
DEPCAT 1	0	(0)	Class I	20	(7.4)
DEPCAT 2	6	(1.9)	Class II	87	(32.2)
DEPCAT 3	19	(6.2)	Class IIIN	32	(11.9)
DEPCAT 4	67	(21.8)	Class IIIM	82	(30.4)
DEPCAT 5	106	(34.4)	Class IV	36	(13.3)
DEPCAT 6	71	(23.1)	Class V	13	(4.8)
DEPCAT 7	39	(12.7)	No occupation given	38	(–)
Category F ('Striving' ACORN) neighbourhood type (> 38)				220	(51.6)
Parental home within a Social Inclusion Partnership area (SIP)				126	(40.9)

Notes: The above figures refer to data collected while respondents were at school in spring 1999.

[a] Social class percentages exclude the 12.3% respondents who could not provide a parental occupation.

	n	(%)		*n*	(%)
Lives in parental home	215	(69.8)	Lives in halls of residence	12	(3.9)
Lives in student flat	30	(9.7)	Lives in private rented flat	36	(11.7)
Council tenant	8	(2.6)	Owner occupier	5	(1.6)
Other	2	(0.6)			
Full use of a car	110	(36.1)	Occasional car access	43	(14.1)
Income from family	95	(31.4)	Income from work	228	(74.3)
Income from bursary	31	(10.1)	Other income	41	(13.4)
Income from loan	143	(46.7)			

Note: The figures below refer to data collected during the final follow up survey of October 2001.

Appendix D: Subjects studied

Subject	1999		2000		2001	
Accounts	7	(4)	8	(5)	4	(4)
Agriculture	2	(0)	2	(0)	0	(0)
Archaeology	1	(1)	0	(0)	0	(0)
Architecture	3	(2)	1	(1)	1	(1)
Art	15	(4)	15	(9)	14	(9)
Astronomy	0	(0)	0	(0)	0	(0)
Beauty	0	(0)	1	(0)	2	(0)
Biology	9	(8)	1	(9)	11	(11)
Build/Survey	4	(1)	3	(2)	2	(2)
Business	23	(17)	28	(17)	17	(14)
Care	9	(0)	7	(0)	6	(0)
Chemistry	9	(9)	11	(11)	7	(7)
Classics	0	(0)	0	(0)	0	(0)
Combined	17	(10)	12	(7)	7	(1)
Compute/IT	11	(6)	10	(7)	4	(4)
Cookery	0	(0)	0	(0)	0	(0)
Dentistry	0	(0)	1	(1)	1	(1)
Divinity	0	(0)	0	(0)	0	(0)
Drama	5	(2)	4	(1)	3	(2)
Economics	0	(0)	2	(2)	3	(3)
Education	9	(9)	8	(8)	9	(9)
Engineering	25	(20)	23	(16)	19	(18)
English	4	(4)	4	(4)	4	(3)
Geography	1	(1)	1	(1)	2	(2)
History	3	(3)	4	(4)	4	(4)
Journalism	5	(1)	4	(1)	3	(1)
Languages	1	(1)	2	(2)	3	(3)
Law	9	(8)	8	(8)	10	(10)
Maths	10	(10)	11	(11)	11	(11)
Medicine	6	(6)	4	(4)	3	(3)
Music	1	(0)	1	(0)	2	(0)
Nautical	0	(0)	0	(0)	0	(0)
Nursing	12	(4)	14	(2)	18	(4)
Optical	1	(0)	2	(1)	1	(0)
Philosophy	0	(0)	0	(0)	0	(0)
Physics	5	(4)	5	(5)	4	(4)
Politics	1	(1)	0	(0)	2	(2)
Psychology	4	(4)	6	(6)	6	(6)
Secretarial	2	(0)	0	(0)	0	(0)
Sociology	0	(0)	0	(0)	1	(1)
Sport	7	(3)	6	(3)	9	(5)
Statistics	0	(0)	1	(1)	1	(1)
Technical	1	(0)	0	(0)	0	(0)
Tourism	9	(4)	6	(2)	4	(2)
Veterinary medicine	0	(0)	0	(0)	0	(0)
Veterinary nursing	1	(0)	1	(0)	0	(0)

Note: Figures in brackets are Degree courses.

Appendix E: Institutions attended

Institution	1999	2000	2001
Glasgow U	32	33	34
Edinburgh U	2	2	2
Aberdeen U	3	1	1
St Andrews U	1	2	1
Strathclyde U	42	42	42
Heriot-Watt U	4	4	4
Dundee U	2	3	3
Stirling U	10	10	10
Caledonian U	34	36	30
Napier U	3	3	2
Robert Gordon U	3	4	4
Abertay U	1	0	1
Paisley U	10	11	17
Glasgow Art HE	0	1	1
Scot. Music/Drama HE	0	1	0
Edinburgh Art HE	0	0	0
Scot. Agricultural HE	1	1	1
Queen Margaret HE	1	1	1
Northern HE	1	1	1
Anniesland FE	2	2	1
Building/Printing FE	6	4	2
Cardonald FE	9	5	2
Central Commerce FE	7	6	1
Food Technology FE	4	1	0
Glasgow Nautical FE	2	1	1
Langside FE	5	4	1
North Glasgow FE	3	1	3
Stow FE	2	2	0
Coatbridge FE	4	5	2
Motherwell FE	3	2	1
Bell FE	8	10	10
Ayr FE	16	12	8
Kilmarnock FE	5	6	4
James Watt FE	3	3	3
Reid Kerr FE	1	0	0
Falkirk FE	0	0	1
Aberdeen FE	0	1	1
Oatridge FE	1	1	0
Scotland Total	231	222	193
'Oxbridge' U	0	0	0
UK 'ivy league' U	0	0	0
UK 'red brick' U	0	0	0
UK 'new' U	4	4	3
UK other HE	1	1	1
UK FE College	1	1	1
Overseas HE/FE	0	0	0
Non-Scottish total	6	6	5

Note: 'Ivy league' universities are represented in bold type, 'red brick' universities by underlining and the 'new' (former polytechnic) universities by italics.

Appendix F: Types of reduced participation

Subject group	Complete	Dropout	Return	Repeat	Restart
Medicine	0	1	0	0	1
Health and welfare	4	4	1	0	2
Science	3	2	1	1	1
Engineering and technology	2	5	2	0	4
Built environment	0	3	1	0	2
Maths and statistics	0	1	0	1	2
Computing and IT	1	3	0	0	0
Catering and hospitality	3	3	2	1	0
Business and administration	8	4	0	0	1
Social sciences	2	4	2	2	0
Humanity and communication	1	1	1	0	0
Art and design	4	3	4	0	0
Education	0	1	0	0	1

Institution	Complete	Dropout	Return	Repeat	Restart
Glasgow U	0	3	1	2	5
Strathclyde U	0	3	1	1	2
Caledonian U	0	9	3	0	3
Other 'ivy league' U	0	1	0	0	2
Other 'red brick' U	0	1	1	0	0
Other 'new' U	0	2	1	1	1
FE college	28	16	7	1	1

Reason	Complete	Dropout	Return	Repeat	Restart
Ended/Qualified	24	1	0	0	0
Not like course	1	9	2	0	12
Not afford course	5	1	2	0	0
Lure of employment	4	4	0	0	0
Health problems	0	5	0	2	0
Loss of motivation	1	4	0	0	2
Stress/Depression	0	2	1	1	2
Personal problems	1	5	0	0	0
Poor course choice	0	4	2	0	0
Poor teaching	0	5	0	0	0
Not clever/Fail	1	1	1	2	0
Year out/Suspended	0	3	1	0	0
Debt	1	2	0	0	0
Gone part time	0	2	0	0	0
Not want course	0	2	0	0	0
Travel	0	1	0	0	0
Other reason	1	1	1	0	0

Notes: Some respondents cited more than one of the above reasons. In all of the above only the repeats are still in these courses. All of the above only refers to their last change in status, some had reduced more than once.

Appendix G: Selection of interviewees

Definition	Category	Questionnaires		Interviews[a]			
		2000	2001	2001		2002	
Never students	–	48	48	–		–	
Former students who failed to complete a course advance to a new course	Dropouts	16	35	11	(12)	7	(10)
Former students who completed a course, but did not advance to a new course	Completers	19	28	5	(5)	2	(4)
Former students who become new students after spending time in the labour market	Returners	2	14	1	(1)	4	(4)
Students who repeat a year or more of study in the same course	Repeaters	9	5	5	(8)	3	(3)
Students who switch to the start of a new course without spending time in the labour market	Restarts	14	14	3	(4)	2	(3)
New students who were in the labour market at Time 1	Deferrers	17	20	2	(3)	3	(4)
Students who completed a course, then advanced to new course	Progressers	66	38	4	(4)	6	(6)
Students who have always been in same (Degree) course	Straight-to-Degree	128	106	9	(9)	14	(14)
Total		**319**	**308**	**40**		**41**	

Note: [a] Figures in brackets are the total number of interviewees who had ever (ie including previously) been in each category.

Appendix H: Profiles of 2001 interviewees

ID	Gender/ Age	Study area	Current residence	DEPCAT	SIP area	Acorn area	Social class	Highers points	Status at time of interview
Muneer	F/19	Glasgow	parental home	6	yes	52	I	48 (30)	'restarter'
Rachel	F/19	Lanark	parental home	6	no	41	II	30 (30)	'restarter'
Malcolm	M/19	Lanark	private flat	5	yes	51	II	40 (28)	'straight-to'
Elspeth	F/19	Argyll	student halls	4	no	2	II	28 (24)	'starter'
Kathleen	F/19	Lanark	parental home	5	yes	50	IV	30 (20)	'completer'
Pierce	M/19	Argyll	student halls	4	no	39	IV	19 (19)	'repeater'
Kayley	F/19	Argyll	student flat	4	yes	51	II	24 (18)	'straight-to'
Felicia	F/19	Ayr	student halls	5	no	30	IIIM	22 (18)	'restarter'
Laurie	F/20	Ayr	parental home	6	no	15	IIIM	22 (18)	'straight-to'
Sheena	F/19	Lanark	parental home	6	yes	42	V	22 (16)	'repeater'
Cyril	M/19	Lanark	parental home	6	no	31	II	22 (15)	'dropout'
Joe	M/19	Lanark	parental home	5	no	43	I	18 (14)	'dropout'
Jock	M/19	Ayr	parental home	5	yes	42	II	15 (14)	'repeater'
Kirsten	F/19	Argyll	parental home	4	no	27	IIIM	17 (13)	'dropout'
Archie	M/19	Glasgow	parental home	6	yes	51	IV	22 (12)	'repeater'
Gregor	M/19	Ayr	student halls	5	no	27	II	22 (12)	'starter'
Catriona	F/19	Argyll	student flat	4	no	7	IIIN	18 (12)	'straight-to'
Noreen	F/19	Lanark	parental home	6	yes	45	II	18 (10)	'straight-to'
Elliot	M/19	Argyll	student flat	4	no	7	X	14 (10)	'straight-to'
Cecilia	F/19	Ayr	student flat	5	yes	40	IIIM	11 (9)	'straight-to'
Chin-Ho	F/19	Ayr	parental home	5	no	26	II	18 (8)	'progresser'
George	M/19	Glasgow	parental home	6	yes	51	IIIM	14 (8)	'dropout'
Ben	M/20	Glasgow	parental home	6	no	40	IIIM	20 (7)	'straight-to'
Vivian	F/19	Lanark	parental home	4	no	14	IIIM	14 (6)	'dropout'
Arlene	F/19	Lanark	parental home	5	no	42	IIIM	14 (6)	'dropout'
Penny	F/19	Ayr	parental home	5	no	42	II	8 (4)	'progresser'
Nell	F/19	Lanark	parental home	6	yes	34	IIIN	9 (2)	'straight-to'
Sinclair	M/19	Ayr	parental home	5	no	30	IIIM	8 (2)	'repeater'
Sammy	M/19	Lanark	parental home	5	no	15	I	4 (2)	'dropout'
Lena	F/18	Argyll	parental home	4	no	6	X	3 (2)	'completer'
Lilly	F/19	Lanark	parental home	6	no	50	II	2 (2)	'completer'
Jean	F/18	Glasgow	parental home	4	no	35	X	10 (0)	'dropout'
Angus	M/19	Ayr	parental home	5	yes	39	V	6 (0)	'dropout'
Callum	M/19	Glasgow	parental home	4	no	28	IIIM	4 (0)	'returner'
Frances	F/19	Ayr	parental home	5	no	50	IIIM	2 (0)	'progresser'
Glenn	M/19	Ayr	parental home	2	no	33	II	2 (0)	'completer'
Lara	F/19	Glasgow	parental home	7	yes	51	IIIM	0 (0)	'dropout'
Jinty	F/19	Argyll	student flat	4	no	33	IIIM	0 (0)	'progresser'
Trevor	M/19	Lanark	parental home	5	no	45	IIIM	0 (0)	'dropout'
Winnie	F/19	Argyll	parental home	4	no	7	X	0 (0)	'completer'

Notes: X = No social class as no parental occupation provided. Figures in brackets are Highers points at S5.

Appendix H: Profiles of 2001 interviewees contd.../

ID	Course or occupation on leaving school (October 1999)	Course or occupation on follow up (October 2000)	Course or occupation on follow up (October 2001)
Muneer	Y1, Architect, Ivy U	Y1, Maths, Ivy U	Y2, Maths, Ivy U
Rachel	Y1, Maths, Ivy U	Y1, Engineering, Ivy U	Y2, Engineering, Ivy U
Malcolm	Y1, Law, Ivy U	Y2, Law, Ivy U	Y3, Law, Ivy U
Elspeth	part-time employment	Y1, English, Ivy U	Y2, English, Ivy U
Kathleen	NC, Art, FE college (a)	part-time employment	HNC, English, FE college (b)
Pierce	Y1, Biology, Ivy U	Y1, Biology, Ivy U	-
Kayley	Y1, Maths, Red U	Y2, Maths, Red U	Y3, Maths, Red U
Felicia	Y1, Engineering, Red U	Y1, Physics, Red U	HND, Combined, FE college
Laurie	Y1, Language, Red U	Y2, Combined, Red U	Y3, Combined, Red U
Sheena	Y1, Education, Ivy U	Y1, Education, Ivy U	-
Cyril	Y1, Account, New U	Y1, Account, New U	full-time employment
Joe	Y1, Computing, Red U	part-time employment	full-time employment
Jock	Y1, Engineering, Ivy U	Y1, Engineering, Ivy U	Y2, Engineering, Ivy U
Kirsten	Y1 Nursing, New U	part-time employment	full-time employment
Archie	Y1, English, Ivy U	Y1, English, Ivy U	full-time employment
Gregor	full-time employment	Y1, Business, Ivy U	Y2, Economics, Ivy U
Catriona	Y1, History, Red U	Y2, History, Red U	Y3, History, Red U
Noreen	Y1, Education, Ivy U	Y2, Education, Ivy U	Y3, Education, Ivy U
Elliot	Y1, Maths, Red U	Y2, Maths, Red U	Y3, Maths, Red U
Cecilia	Y1, History, Red U	Y2, History, Red U	Y3, History, Red U
Chin-Ho	HND, Biology, Red U	HND, Biology, Red U	Y3, Biology, Red U
George	Y1, Tourism, New U	Y1, Tourism, New U	HND, Tourism, FE college
Ben	Y1, Building, New U	Y2, Building, New U	-
Vivian	Y1, Biology, New U	HND, Optical, New U	full-time employment
Arlene	Y1, Tourism, New U	full-time employment	full-time employment
Penny	NC, Art, FE college	HNC, Art, FE college	-
Nell	Y1, Psychology, New U	Y2, Psychology, New U	Y3, Psychology, New U
Sinclair	Y1, Art, Red U	Y1, Art, Red U	HNC, Art, FE college
Sammy	HND, Business, FE college	full-time employment	-
Lena	NC, Nursing, FE college	full-time employment	HND, Nursing, New U
Lilly	NC, Art, FE college	full-time employment	full-time employment
Jean	returned to school	Y1, Combined, New U (a)	Y1, Drama, New U (b)
Angus	NC, Art, FE college	NC, Art, FE college	unemployed
Callum	HND, Building, FE college	Highers, FE college	Y1, Law, New U
Frances	NC, Business, FE college	HND, Business, FE college	HND, Business, FE college
Glenn	Highers, FE college	full-time employment	-
Lara	NC, Care, FE college	training scheme	full-time employment
Jinty	HNC, Tourism, FE college	HND, Tourism, FE college	full-time employment
Trevor	HND, Nursing, FE college	part-time employment	full-time employment
Winnie	NC, Art, FE college	unemployed	unemployed

Notes: Y1 = first year, Y2 = second year, Y3 = third year of Degree courses (only).

Ivy U = ancient or 'ivy league' university; Red U = established or 'red brick' university; New U = former polytechnic or 'new' university; FE college = further education college.

Appendix I: Profiles of 2002 interviewees

ID	Gender/ Age	Study area	Current residence	DEPCAT	SIP area	Acorn area	Social class	Highers points	Status at time of interview
Ailsa	F/20	Ayr	home owner	5	no	45	II	42 (30)	'starter'
Jessie	F/20	Argyll	private flat	4	no	7	II	30 (30)	'dropout'
Ellen	F/20	Glasgow	parental home	4	no	15	II	34 (28)	'straight-to'
Colleen	F/20	Argyll	private flat	6	no	7	II	36 (26)	'straight-to'
Jack	M/20	Argyll	private flat	4	yes	49	IIIN	27 (26)	'straight-to'
Crissy	F/20	Glasgow	parental home	6	yes	51	II	30 (24)	'straight-to'
Rab	M/20	Glasgow	parental home	7	no	42	IV	24 (24)	'straight-to'
Sorley	M/20	Argyll	private flat	2	no	7	IIIM	34 (22)	'straight-to'
Johnny	M/20	Glasgow	parental home	7	yes	51	X	24 (20)	'straight-to'
Annie	F/20	Glasgow	parental home	6	yes	49	X	28 (18)	'restarter'
Logan	F/20	Ayr	parental home	6	yes	50	IIIM	22 (18)	'repeater'
Dorothy	F/20	Ayr	private flat	6	no	6	V	21 (18)	'progresser'
Edith	F/20	Argyll	parental home	4	no	39	IIIM	18 (16)	'returner'
Charlotte	F20	Glasgow	parental home	6	yes	42	IIIM	22 (15)	'repeater'
Donald	M/20	Argyll	private flat	3	no	7	II	22 (15)	'straight-to'
Christel	F/20	Glasgow	parental home	7	yes	51	X	18 (14)	'straight-to'
Jimmy	M/20	Lanark	parental home	5	yes	49	IIIN	25 (13)	'restarter'
Evelyn	F/20	Glasgow	home owner	7	yes	51	IV	22 (12)	'dropout'
Fergus	M/20	Lanark	private flat	5	yes	43	II	18 (12)	'straight-to'
Lucy	F/20	Argyll	private flat	3	no	7	IIIM	14 (12)	'starter'
Patricia	F/20	Ayr	parental home	5	no	6	X	20 (10)	'completer'
Lexy	F/20	Lanark	council tenant	5	yes	41	IIIN	16 (10)	'returner'
Dougie	M/20	Argyll	student halls	3	no	3	II	20 (9)	'dropout'
Kylie	F20	Ayr	private flat	5	yes	42	X	15 (9)	'straight-to'
Loretta	F/20	Lanark	parental home	6	yes	51	IIIN	12 (8)	'dropout'
Kieran	M/20	Lanark	parental home	4	yes	43	IIIM	10 (8)	'dropout'
Avril	F/20	Ayr	parental home	6	no	41	IIIN	8 (8)	'completer'
Audrey	F/20	Lanark	parental home	6	no	45	II	19 (7)	'straight-to'
Libby	F20	Glasgow	parental home	6	yes	42	I	6 (6)	'starter'
Flora	F/20	Glasgow	parental home	4	yes	23	IIIM	10 (4)	'returner'
Leonora	F/20	Lanark	parental home	5	yes	42	IV	10 (4)	'progresser'
Prentice	M/20	Ayr	private flat	5	no	45	IIIN	10 (2)	'dropout'
Lizzie	F/20	Glasgow	parental home	7	yes	49	V	8 (2)	'progresser'
Shug	M/19	Glasgow	parental home	6	no	15	II	8 (2)	'progresser'
Emily	F/20	Ayr	private flat	5	yes	38	IV	7 (2)	'straight-to'
Lou	M/20	Lanark	parental home	4	no	14	II	6 (2)	'straight-to'
Bruce	M/20	Lanark	parental home	5	yes	51	X	4 (2)	'returner'
Eleanor	F/20	Argyll	student halls	4	no	43	IIIN	- (1)	'returner'
Patrick	M/19	Glasgow	council tenant	7	yes	40	V	18 (0)	'dropout'
Chad	M/20	Lanark	parental home	6	no	41	II	1 (0)	'progresser'
Morven	F/20	Ayr	parental home	6	no	35	V	0 (0)	'progresser'

Appendix I: Profiles of 2002 interviewees contd.../

ID	Course or occupation on leaving school (October 1999)	Course or occupation on follow up (October 2000)	Course or occupation on follow up (October 2001)
Ailsa	full-time employment	Y1, Accounts, Red U	Y2, Accounts, Red U
Jessie	Y1, Medicine, Ivy U	Y2, Medicine, Ivy U	unemployed
Ellen	Y1, Medicine, Ivy U	Y2, Medicine, Ivy U	Y3, Medicine, Ivy U
Colleen	Y1, Law, Red U	Y2, Law, Red U	Y3, Law, Red U
Jack	Y1, Engineering, Ivy U	Y2, Engineering, Ivy U	Y3, Engineering, Ivy U
Crissy	Y1, Biology, Ivy U	Y2, Biology, Ivy U	Y3, Biology, Ivy U
Rab	Y1, Physics, Ivy U	Y2, Physics, Ivy U	Y3, Physics, Ivy U
Sorley	Y1, Maths, Red U	Y2, Maths, Red U	Y3, Maths, Red U
Johnny	Y1, Computing, Ivy U	Y2, Computing, Ivy U	Y3, Computing, Ivy U
Annie	Y1, Education, Red U	Y1, Languages, Red U	Y2, Languages, Red U
Logan	Y1, Maths, Ivy U	Y2, Maths, Ivy U	Y2, Maths, Ivy U
Dorothy	HND, Art, FE college	HND, Art, FE college	Y3, Art, New U
Edith	Y1, Tourism, New U	full-time employment	Y1, Art, FE college
Charlotte	Y1, Biology, Ivy U	Y2, Biology, Ivy U	Y2, Biology, Ivy U
Donald	Y1, Engineering, Red U	Y2, Engineering, Red U	Y3, Engineering, Red U
Christel	Y1, Psychology, Red U	Y2, Psychology, Red U	Y3, Psychology, Red U
Jimmy	Y1, Engineering, Ivy U	Y1, Building, New U	Y2, Building, New U
Evelyn	Y1, Biology, Ivy U	Y1, Biology, Ivy U	part-time employment
Fergus	Y1, Sports, Red U	Y2, Sports, Red U	Y3, Sports, Red U
Lucy	full-time employment	Y1, Business, New U	Y2, Business, New U
Patricia	HND, Sports, FE college	HND, Sports, FE college	full-time employment
Lexy	Y1, Combined, New U	Y2, Combined, New U	Y2, Combined, New U
Dougie	Y1, Business, Red U	Y2, Business, Red U	part-time employment
Kylie	Y1, Chemistry, New U	Y2, Chemistry, New U	Y3, Maths, New U
Loretta	full-time employment	HND, Drama, FE college	full-time employment
Kieran	Y1, Engineering, New U	part-time employment	part-time employment
Avril	NC, Secretarial, FE college	HNC, Secretarial, FE college	part-time employment
Audrey	Y1, Maths, Red U	Y2, Maths, Red U	Y3, Maths, Red U
Libby	full-time employment	full-time employment	HND, Sports, FE college
Flora	Y1, Drama, New U (a)	Y1, Art, New U (b)	NC, Drama, FE college
Lconora	HND, Journalism, FE college	HND, Journalism, FE college	Y1, English, Ivy U
Prentice	HND, Engineering, FE college	HND, Engineering, FE college	unemployed
Lizzie	HND, Accounts, FE college	HND, Accounts, FE college	Y2, Accounts, New U
Shug	HND, Engineering, FE college	HND, Engineering, FE college	Y3, Engineering, New U
Emily	Y1, Combined, Red U	Y2, Combined, Red U	Y3, Biology, Red U
Lou	Y1, Politics, New U	Y2, Politics, New U	Y3, Politics, New U
Bruce	NC, Art, FE college	full-time employment	HNC, Art, FE college
Eleanor	HND, Journalism, FE college	full-time employment	Y1, English, Red U
Patrick	Y1, Maths, Red U	Y2, Maths, Red U	full-time employment
Chad	HND, Business, FE college	HND, Business, FE college	Y3, Business, New U
Morven	NC, Combined, FE college	HNC, Combined, FE college	Y1, Combined, New U

Notes: Y1 = first year, Y2 = second year, Y3 = third year of Degree courses (only).

Ivy U = ancient or 'ivy league' university; Red U = established or 'red brick' university; New U = former polytechnic or 'new' university; FE college = further education college.

Available from The Policy Press in association with the Joseph Rowntree Foundation

Socioeconomic disadvantage and access to higher education

Alasdair Forsyth and Andy Furlong

Paperback £12.95 ISBN 1 86134 296 9
November 2000

The recent debate concerning elitism in higher education in the UK and the related goal of broadening access has been represented in Scotland by the recent Cubie report into fairness in student finance. *Socioeconomic disadvantage and access to higher education* argues that the gap in representation in higher education between affluent and disadvantaged young people continues. The research looks at reasons for this, but takes care to distinguish between the factors which *qualify* young people for higher education and those which *predispose* them to attend. That is, which factors govern levels of qualification required for entry to higher education and which other factors act as barriers to the progress of disadvantaged young people.

Through a survey of school-leavers, before and after leaving school, the report looks at:

- geographical patterns of academic achievement in relation to indicators of disadvantage;
- the attrition from full-time education of qualified but disadvantaged young people;
- the variety of destinations made by disadvantaged school-leavers;
- patterns and levels of participation in higher and further education;
- student finance and parental support;
- barriers to full participation in higher education.

The report concludes with policy recommendations for increasing meaningful participation for under-represented disadvantaged groups of young people which are applicable throughout the UK.

Socioeconomic disadvantage and access to higher education is vital reading for policy makers and academics in the fields of education, young people and social exclusion, and anyone interested in higher education and youth transitions.

For further information about these and other titles published by The Policy Press, please visit our website at:
www.policypress.org.uk or telephone
+44 (0)117 331 4054

To order, please contact:
Marston Book Services
PO Box 269
Abingdon
Oxon OX14 4YN
UK Tel: +44 (0)1235 465500
Fax: +44 (0)1235 465556
E-mail: direct.orders@marston.co.uk